Ed Sheeran

EQUALS

Album Cover: Zak Walters / Original Artwork: Ed Sheeran / Photography: Zak Walters
Artwork used by permission from Asylum Records UK/Atlantic Records UK

ISBN: 978-1-70515-412-0

Visit Hal Leonard Online at
www.halleonard.com

Contact us:
Hal Leonard
7777 West Bluemound Road
Milwaukee, WI 53213
Email: info@halleonard.com

In Europe, contact:
Hal Leonard Europe Limited
42 Wigmore Street
Marylebone, London, W1U 2RY
Email: info@halleonardeurope.com

In Australia, contact:
Hal Leonard Australia Pty. Ltd.
4 Lentara Court
Cheltenham, Victoria, 3192 Australia
Email: info@halleonard.com.au

T0050644

Ed Sheeran

EQUALS

Contents

Tides

Words and Music by Ed Sheeran, Johnny McDaid and Foy Vance

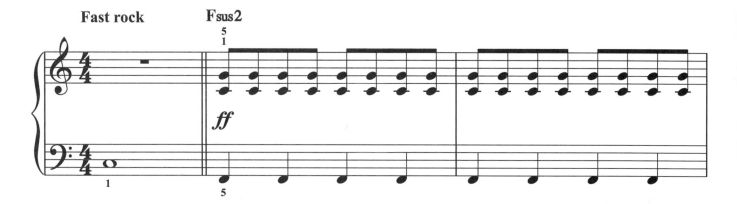

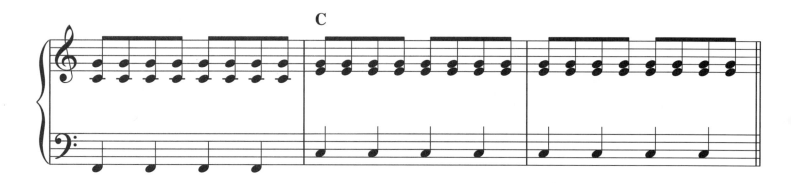

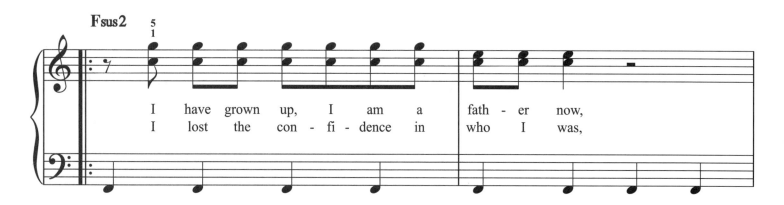

I have grown up, I am a father now,
I lost the con - fi - dence in who I was,

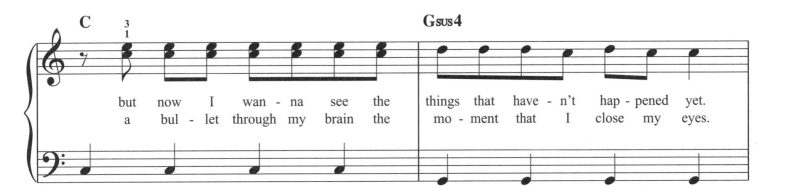

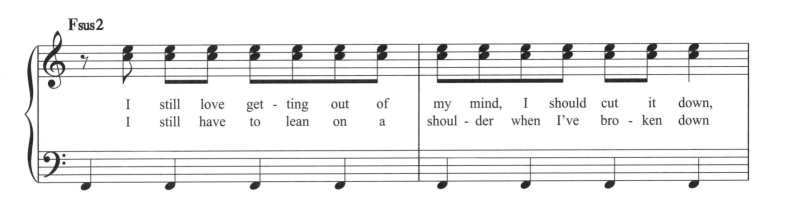

C
Gsus4

I still know peo - ple I don't like and I should cut them out.
and I have peo - ple that de - pend on me to sort them out.

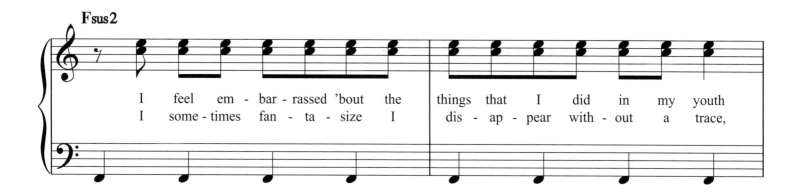

Fsus2

I feel em - bar - rassed 'bout the things that I did in my youth
I some - times fan - ta - size I dis - ap - pear with - out a trace,

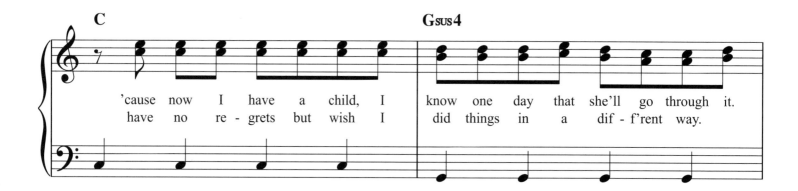

C
Gsus4

'cause now I have a child, I know one day that she'll go through it.
have no re - grets but wish I did things in a dif - f'rent way.

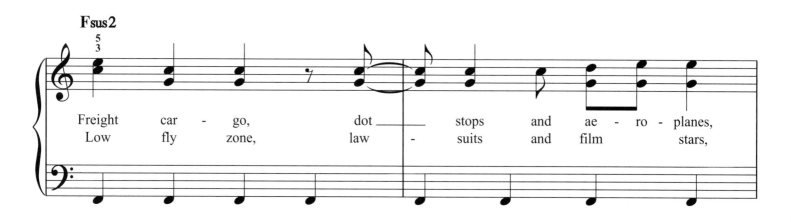

Fsus2

Freight car - go, dot stops and ae - ro - planes,
Low fly zone, law - suits and film stars,

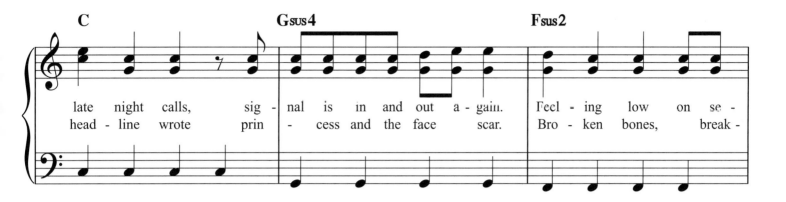

late night calls, sig - nal is in and out a - gain. Feel - ing low on se -
head - line wrote prin - cess and the face scar. Bro - ken bones, break -

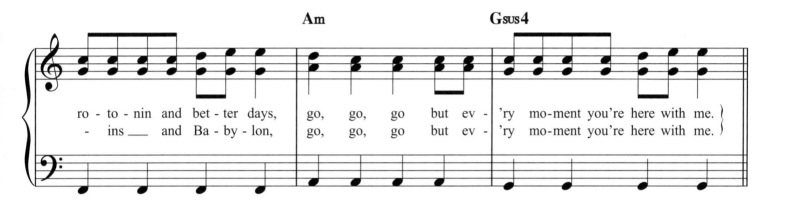

ro - to - nin and bet - ter days, go, go, go but ev - 'ry mo-ment you're here with me.
- ins __ and Ba - by - lon, go, go, go but ev - 'ry mo-ment you're here with me.

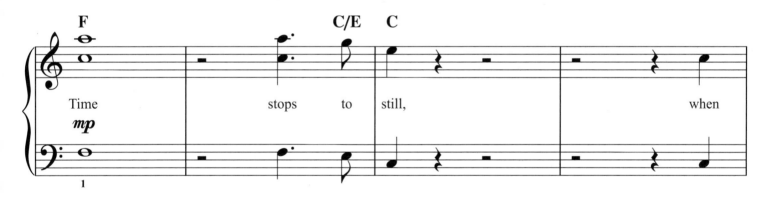

Time stops to still, when

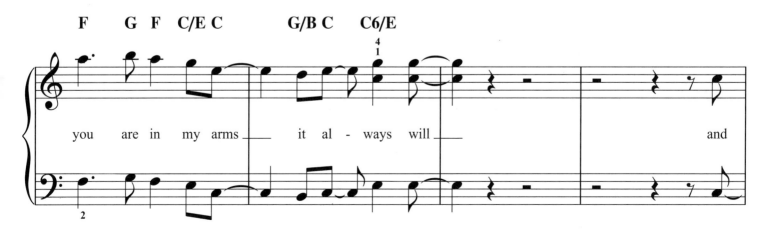

you are in my arms __ it al - ways will __ and

life,   life   is   chang -   ing   tides. __

Time

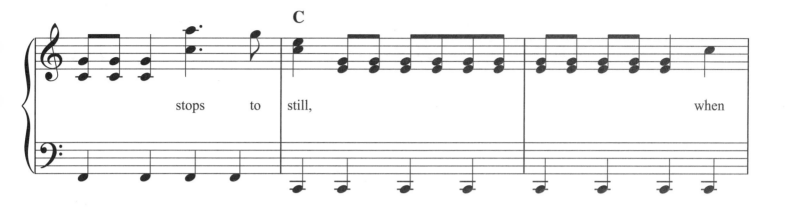

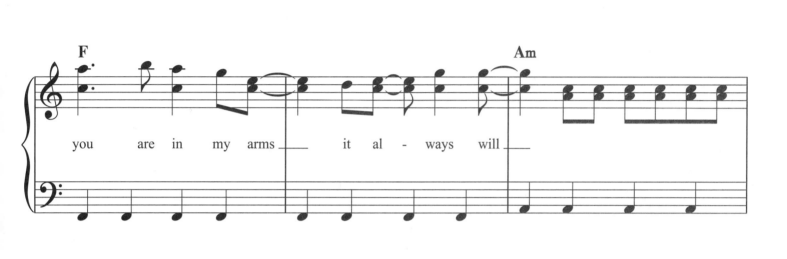

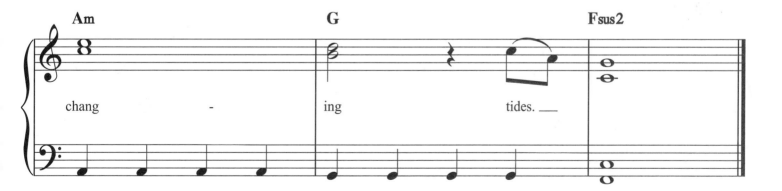

Shivers

Words and Music by Ed Sheeran, Johnny McDaid, Steve Mac and Kal Lavelle

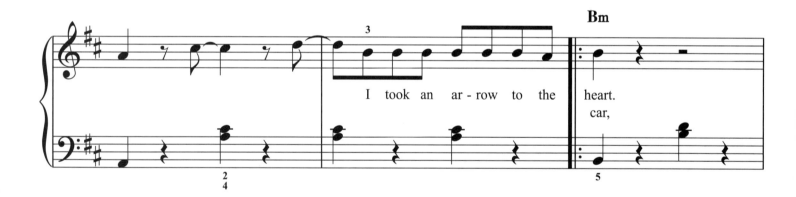

I took an ar-row to the heart.
car,

I nev-er kissed a mouth that taste like yours.
on the back ___ seat in the moon-lit dark.
Straw-ber-ries ___ and
Wrap me up ___ be-tween your

14

ooh,   I love it when you do it like ___ that. And when you're

close   up, ___ give me the shiv - ers.   Oh, ba - by,

you   wan - na dance 'til the sun - light cracks ___ and when they

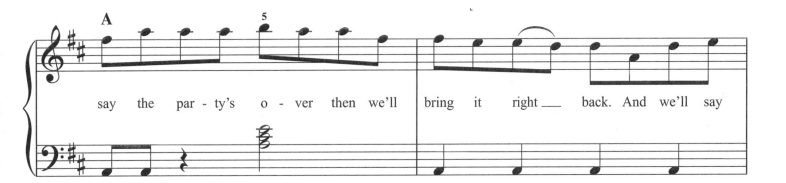

say the par - ty's o - ver then we'll bring it right ___ back. And we'll say

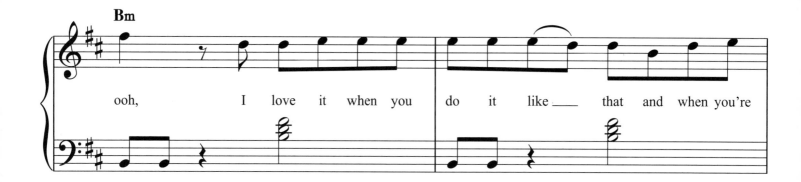

ooh,   I love it when you do it like ___ that and when you're

close up, ___ give me the shiv-ers.   Oh, ba - by,   you wan-na dance 'til the

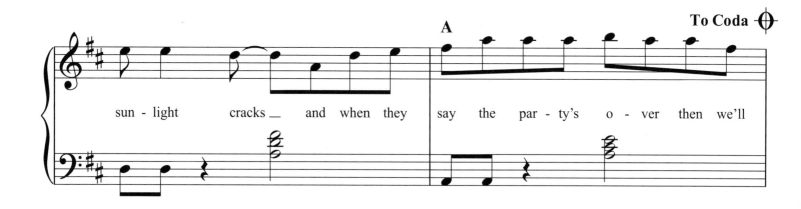

To Coda ⊕

sun - light cracks ___ and when they say the par-ty's o - ver then we'll

1. bring it right ___ back. In - to the

2. bring it right ___ back.   Ba - by,

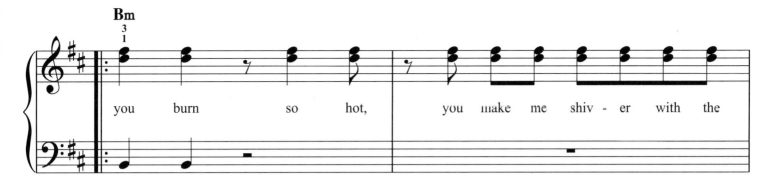

you burn so hot, you make me shiv-er with the

fi - re you got. This thing we start-ed, I don't want it to stop,

you know you make me shiv-er, ___ er, ___ er. ___ Ba - by,

Yeah, ___ you got me sing-ing like ooh, I love it when you

D.S. al Coda

do it like ___ that and when you're

CODA

bring it right ___ back, yeah.

First Times

Words and Music by Ed Sheeran, Fred Gibson and David Hodges

Gentle ballad

I thought it would feel _ dif - f'ent,

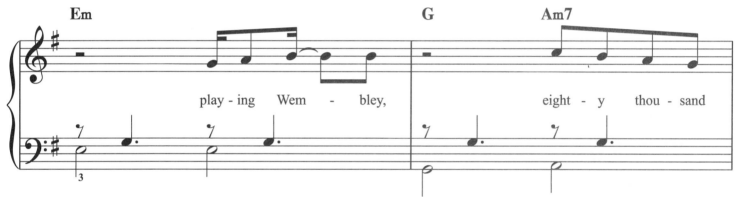

play - ing Wem - bley, eight - y thou - sand

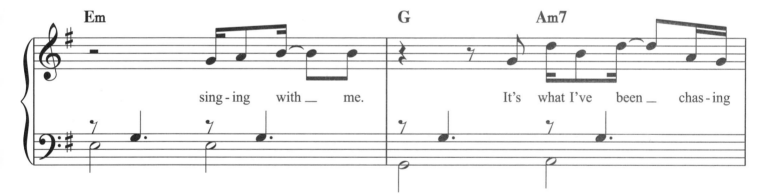

sing - ing with _ me. It's what I've been _ chas - ing

'cause this is the dream.

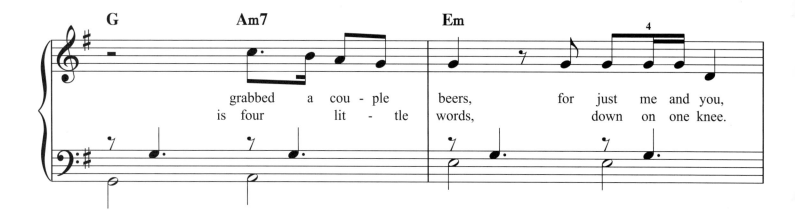

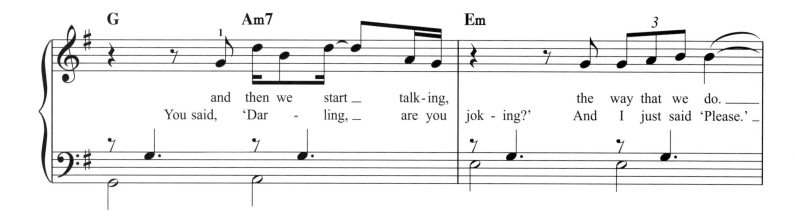

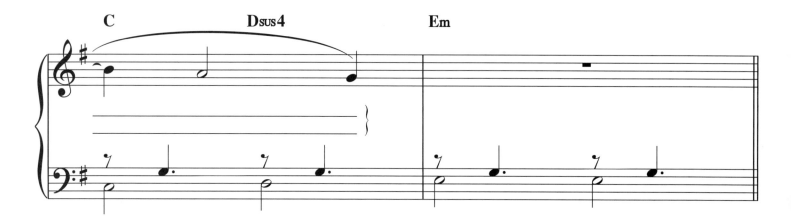

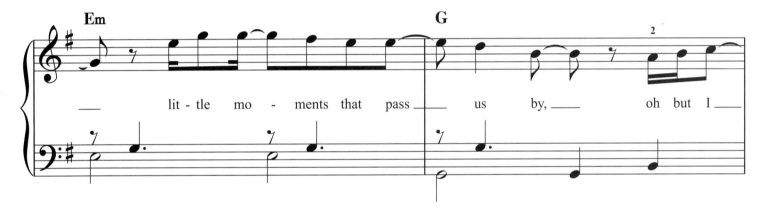

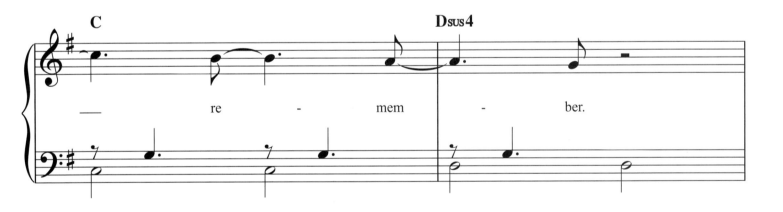

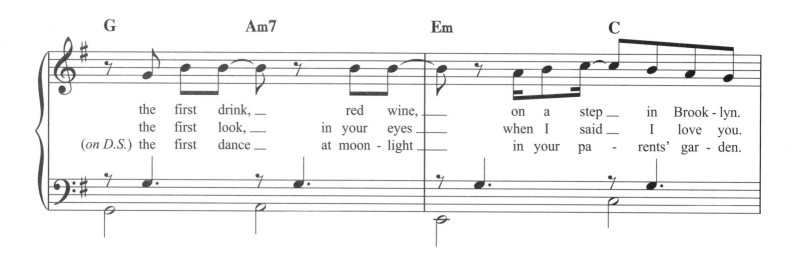

the first drink, ___ red wine, ___ on a step ___ in Brook - lyn.
the first look, ___ in your eyes ___ when I said ___ I love you.
(on D.S.) the first dance ___ at moon - light ___ in your pa - rents' gar - den.

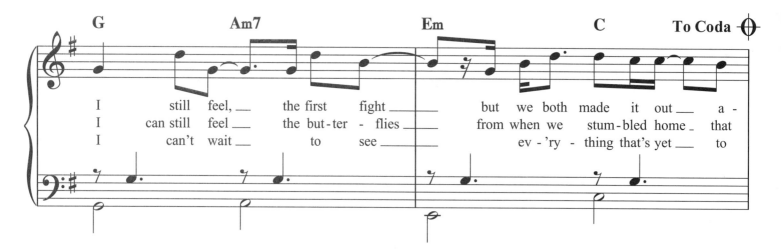

I still feel, ___ the first fight ___ but we both made it out ___ a -
I can still feel ___ the but - ter - flies ___ from when we stum - bled home ___ that
I can't wait ___ to see ___ ev - 'ry - thing that's yet ___ to

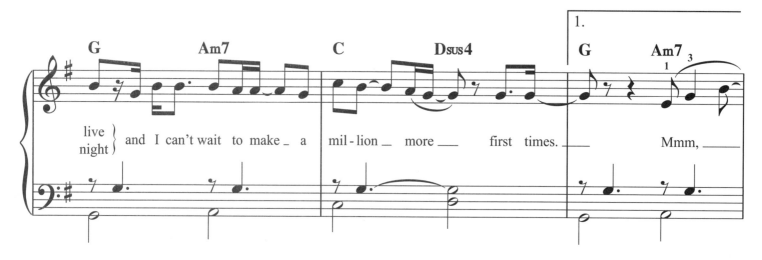

live } and I can't wait to make _ a mil - lion ___ more ___ first times. ___ Mmm, ___
night }

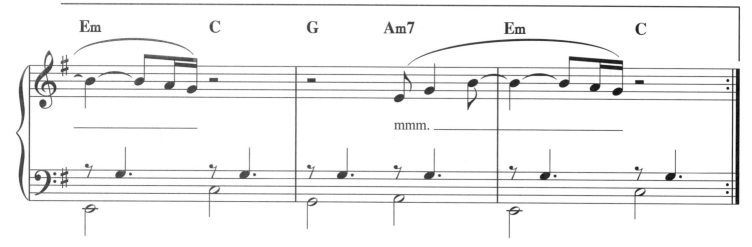

mmm. ___

22

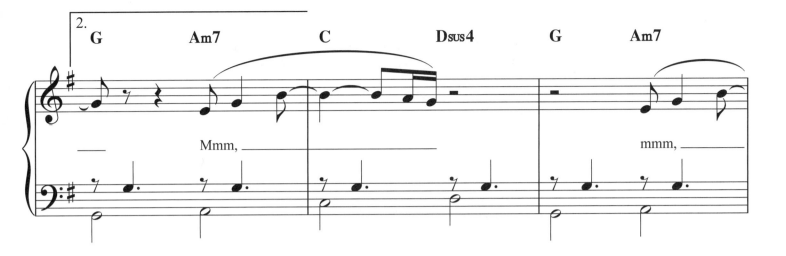

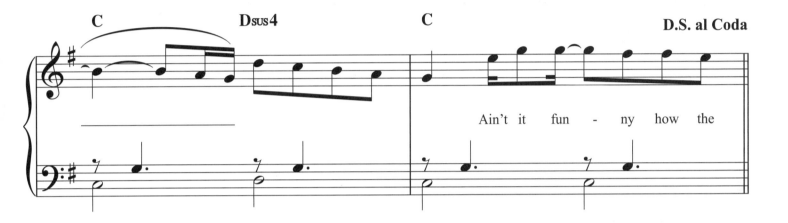

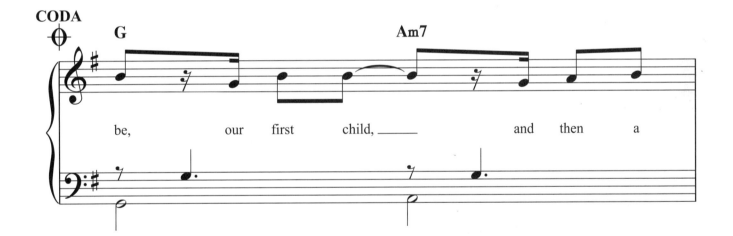

Bad Habits

Words and Music by Ed Sheeran, Johnny McDaid and Fred Gibson

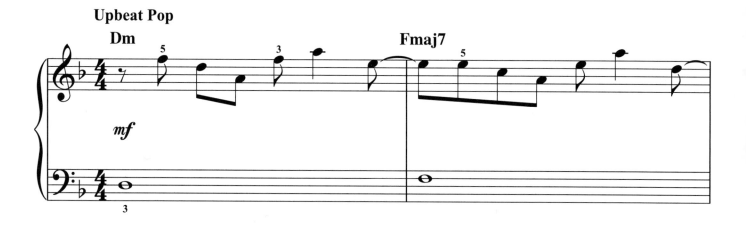

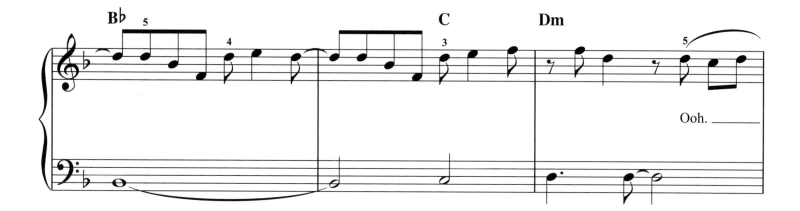

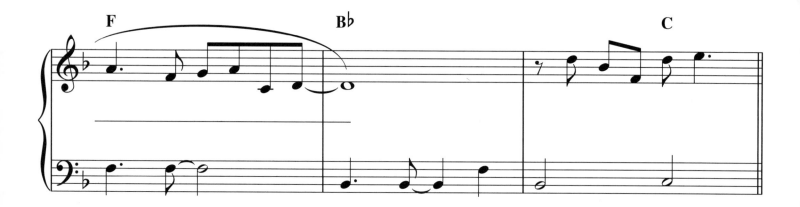

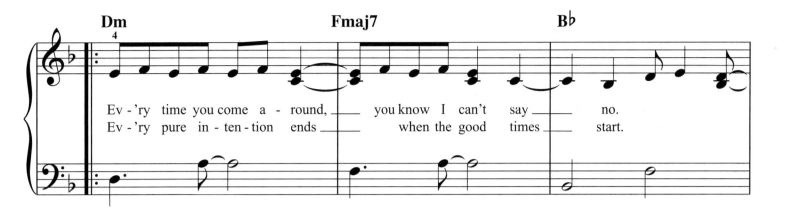

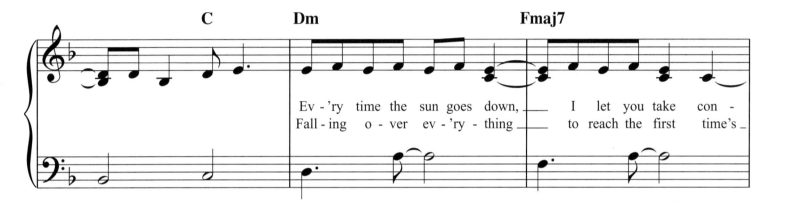

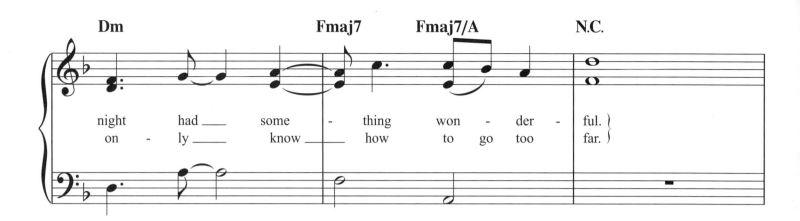

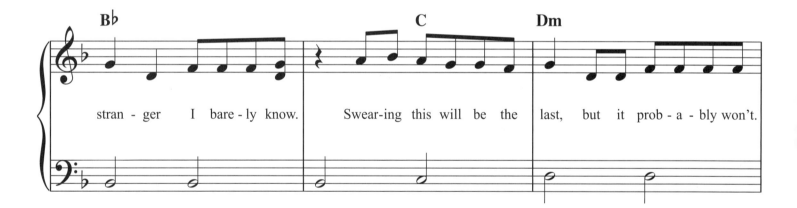

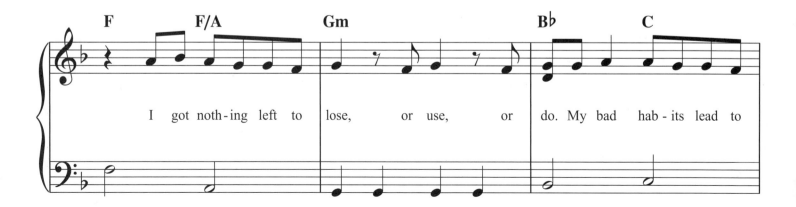

wide eyes star-ing at space, and I know I'll lose con - trol of the things that I say. _

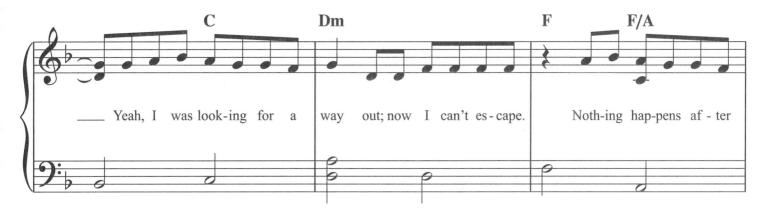

_ Yeah, I was look-ing for a way out; now I can't es - cape. Noth-ing hap-pens af - ter

two. It's true, it's true, my bad hab - its lead to you. Ooh. _____

_____ My bad hab - its lead to

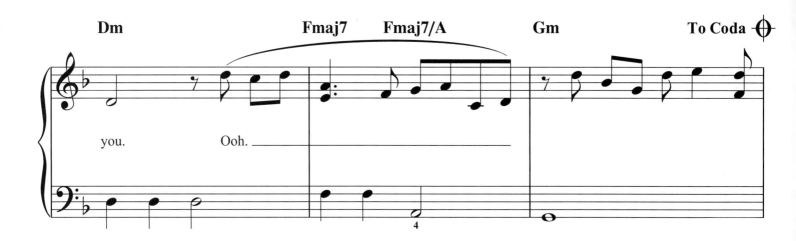

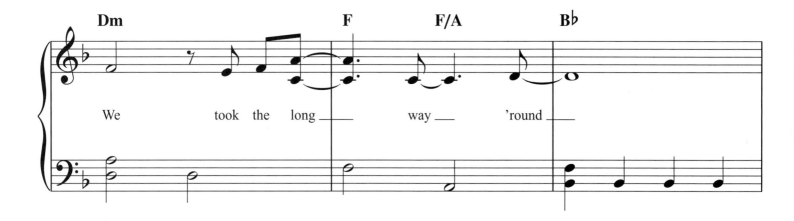

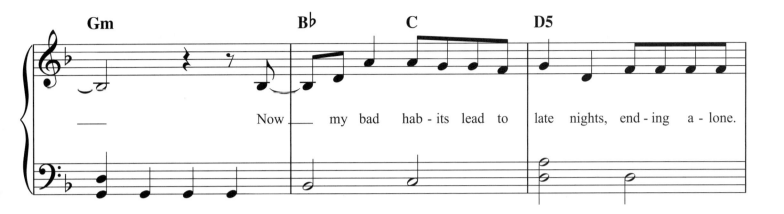

Now ___ my bad hab - its lead to late nights, end - ing a - lone.

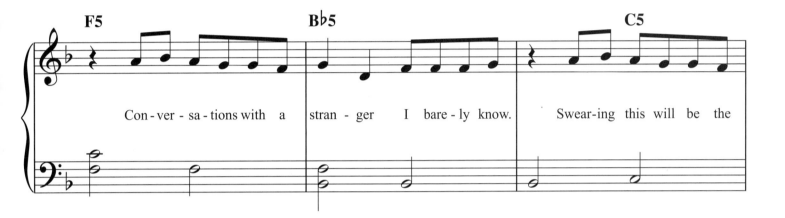

Con - ver - sa - tions with a stran - ger I bare - ly know. Swear-ing this will be the

last, but it prob - a - bly won't. I got noth-ing left to lose, or use, or

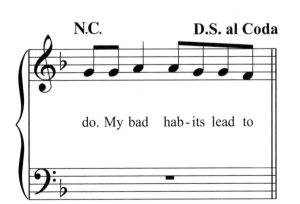

do. My bad hab-its lead to

My bad hab-its lead to you.

Overpass Graffiti

Words and Music by Ed Sheeran, Johnny McDaid and Fred Gibson

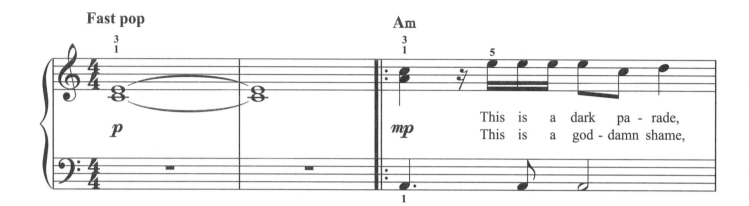

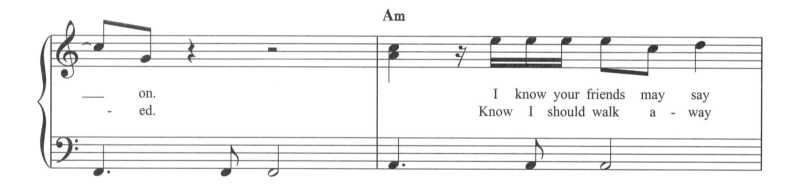

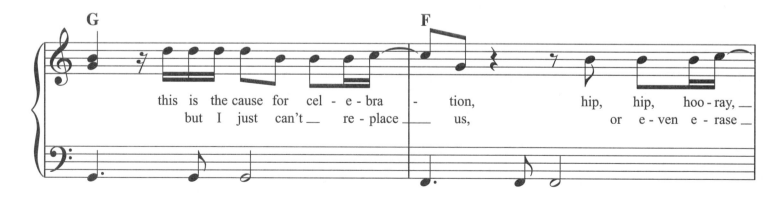

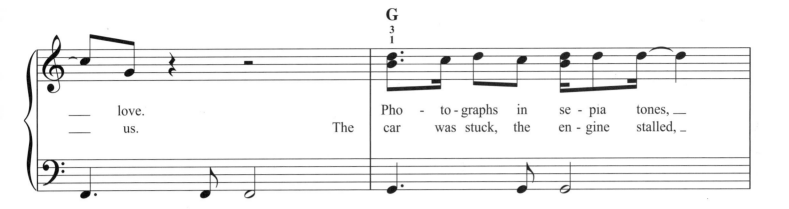

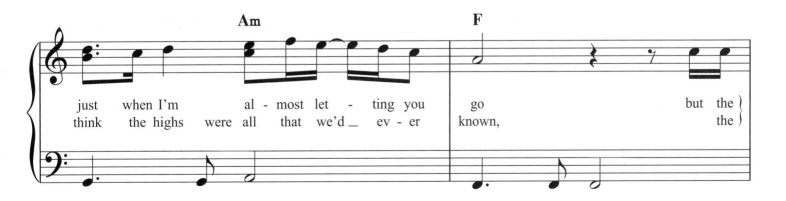

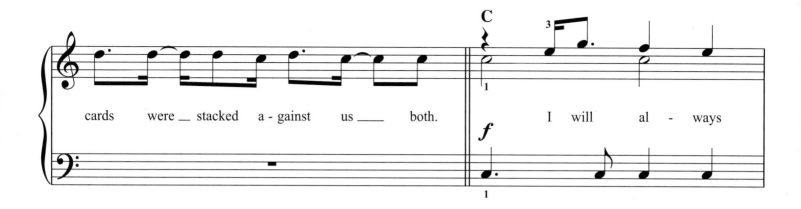

cards were _ stacked a - gainst us _ both.   I will al - ways

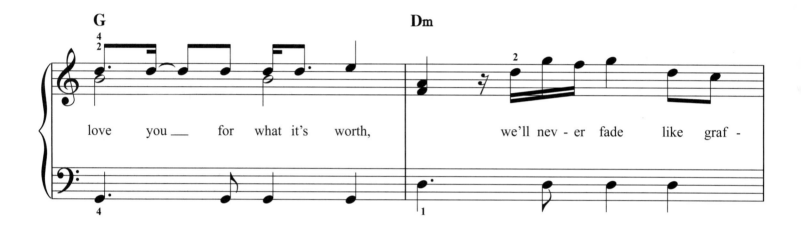

love you _ for what it's worth,   we'll nev - er fade like graf -

fi - ti - on _ the o - ver-pass. _   I know time _ may

change the way you think of us _   but I'll re-mem - ber the way we were. _ You were the

first full stop, love that will nev - er leave _____ and,

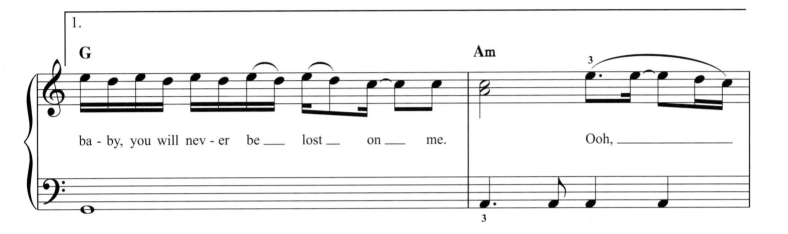

1.

ba - by, you will nev - er be __ lost __ on __ me. Ooh, _____

ooh, _____ ooh. _____

2.

ba - by, you will nev - er be __ lost __ on __ me. Ooh, _____

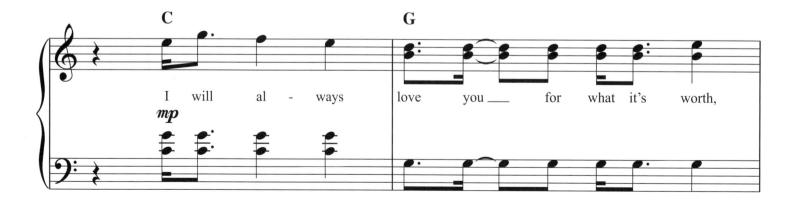

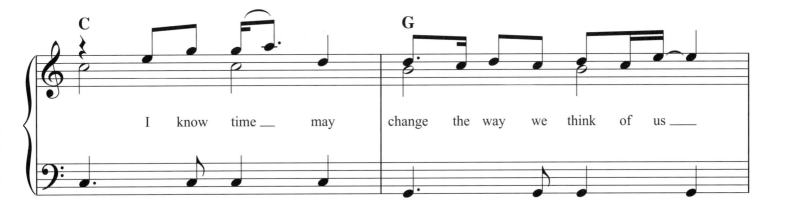

Ooh, _____ Ooh, _____

yeah, ___ yeah, ___ yeah. Yeah, _____ yeah, ___ yeah. Lost on

me. _____ Ooh. _____ Graf-

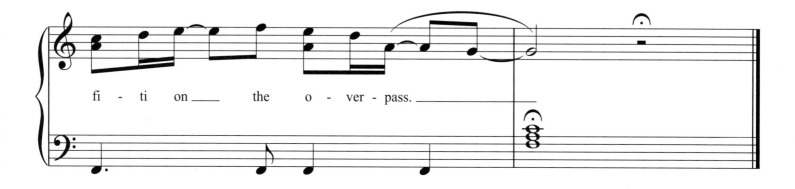

fi - ti on ___ the o - ver - pass. _____

The Joker And The Queen

Words and Music by Ed Sheeran, Samuel Roman, Johnny McDaid and Fred Gibson

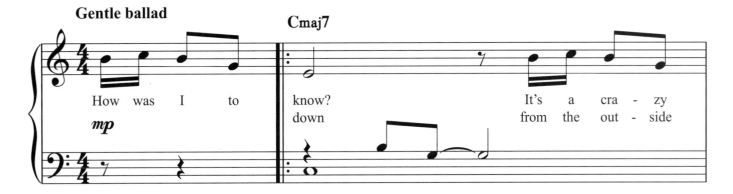

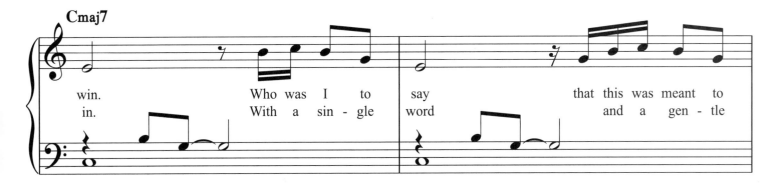

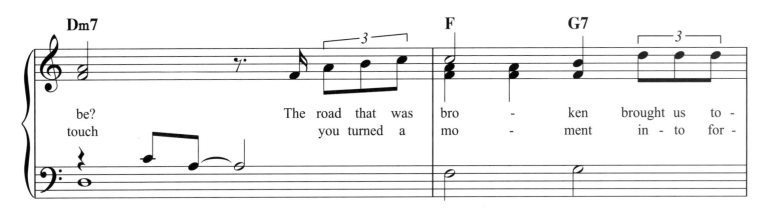

geth - er. _____ } And I know you could fall for a
ev - er. _____

thou - sand kings _____ and hearts that could give you a

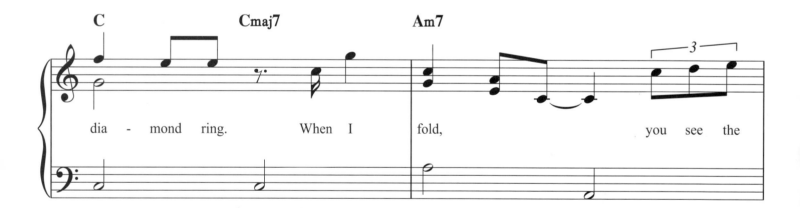

dia - mond ring. When I fold, you see the

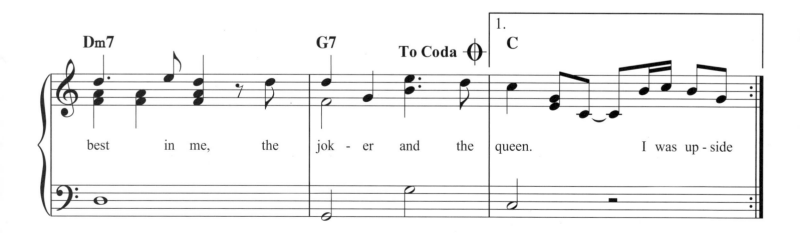

best in me, the jok - er and the queen. I was up - side

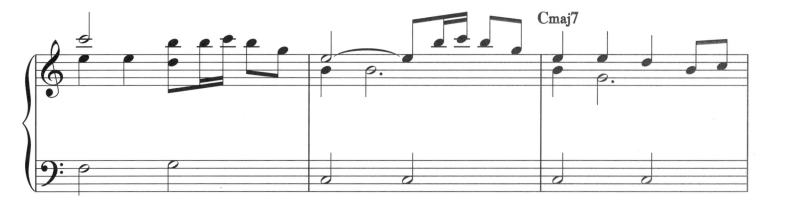

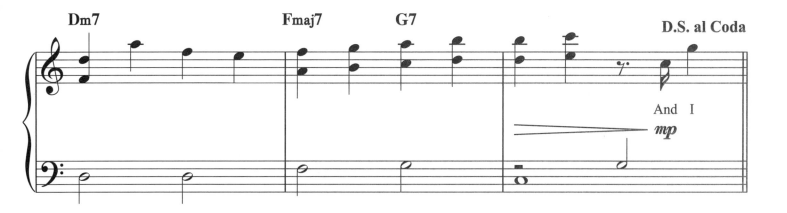

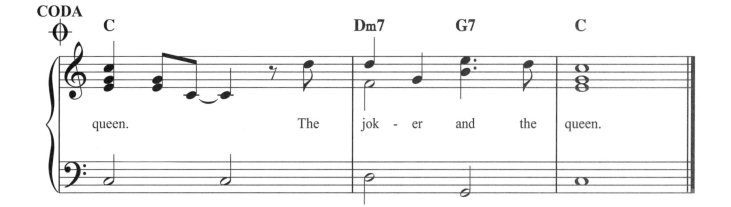

Leave Your Life

Words and Music by Ed Sheeran

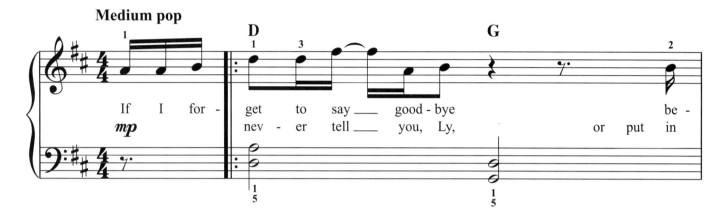

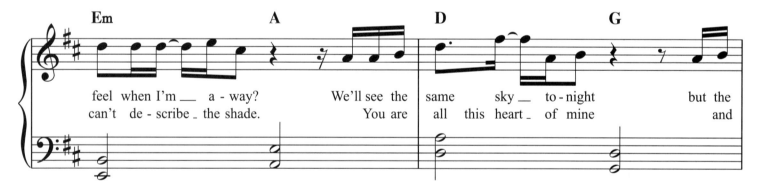

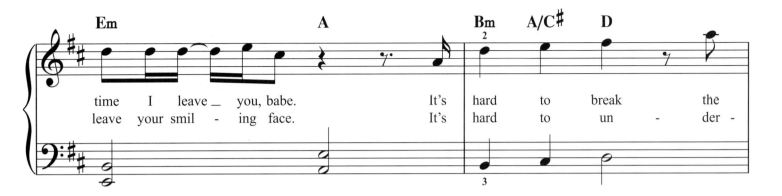

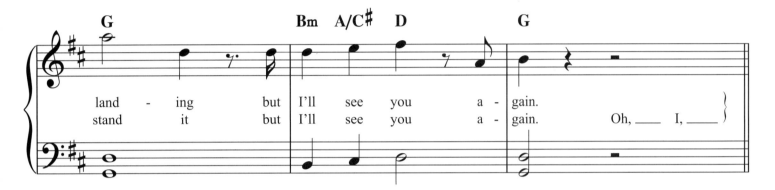

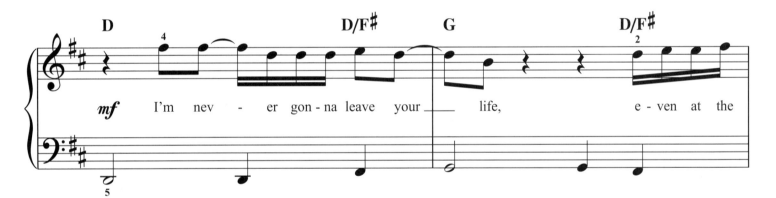

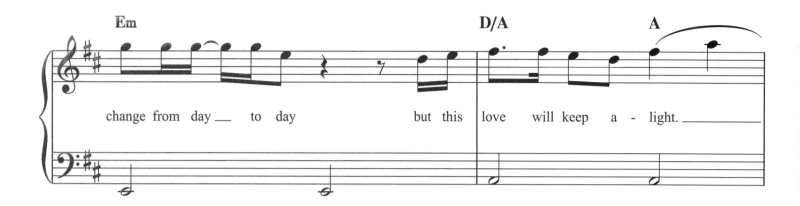

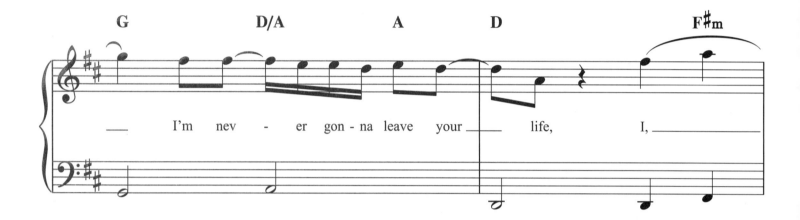

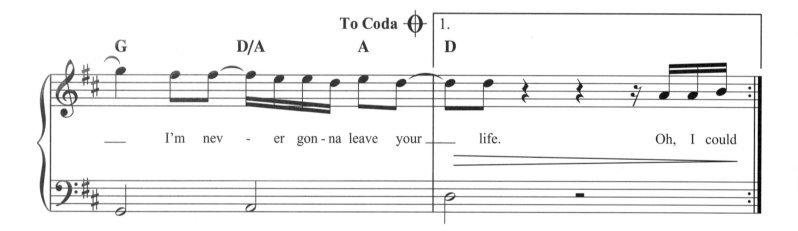

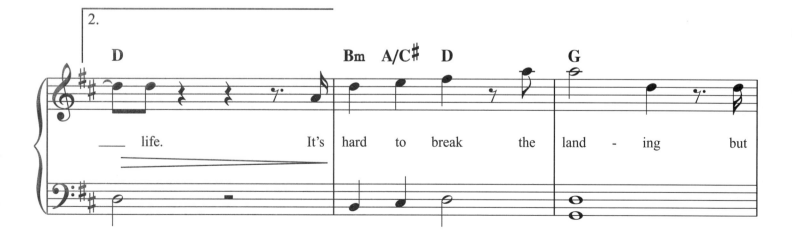

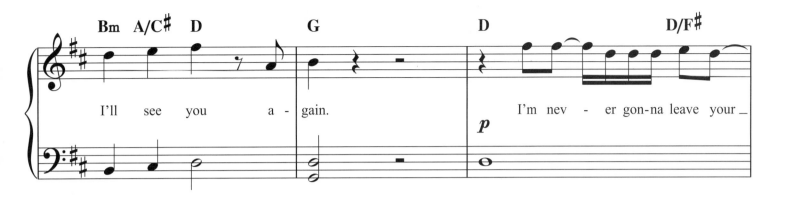

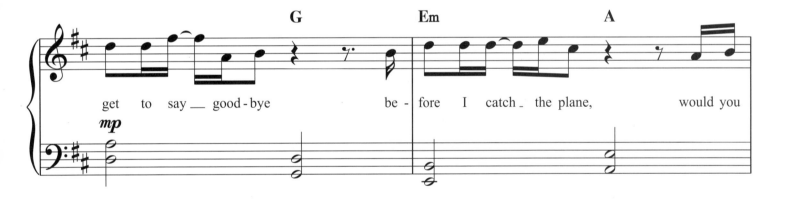

Collide

Words and Music by Ed Sheeran, Johnny McDaid, Fred Gibson and Benjamin Kweller

Oh, yeah, we've been in the rain, ___

been on the rocks but we found ___ our way,

we've or-dered piz-za to an

ae - ro - plane,   slept on the beach like __ we were cast - a - ways.

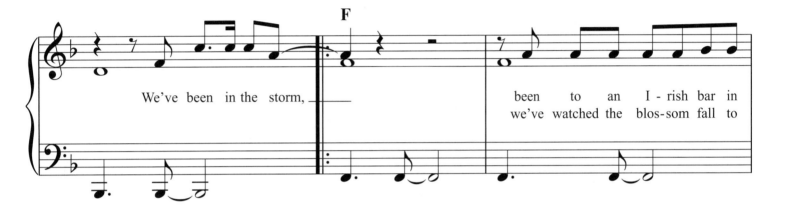

We've been in the storm, _____   been to an I - rish bar in
we've watched the blos-som fall to

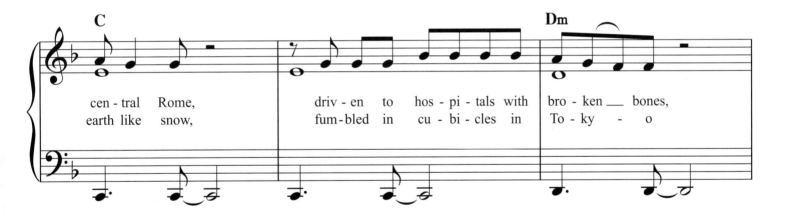

cen - tral Rome,   driv - en to hos - pi - tals with bro - ken __ bones,
earth like snow,   fum-bled in cu - bi - cles in To - ky - o

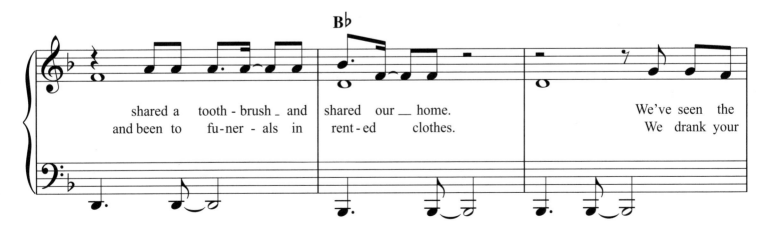

shared a tooth - brush _ and   shared our __ home.   We've seen the
and been to fu-ner - als in   rent - ed clothes.   We drank your

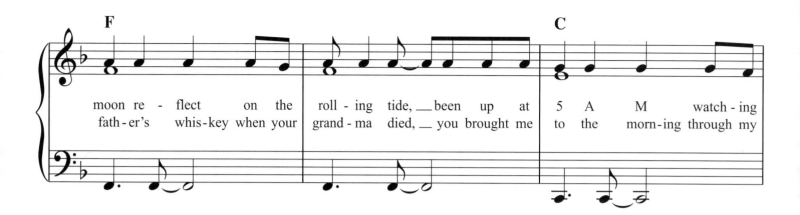

moon re - flect on the | roll - ing tide, __ been up at | 5 A M watch - ing
fath - er's whis-key when your | grand - ma died, __ you brought me | to the morn-ing through my

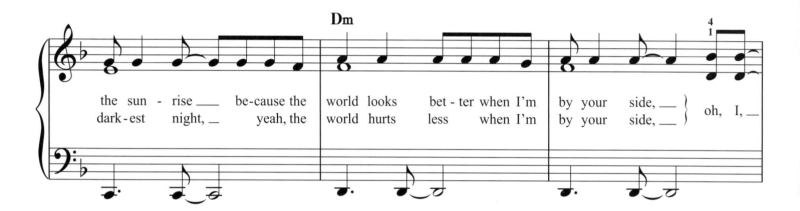

the sun - rise __ be-cause the | world looks bet - ter when I'm | by your side, __ } oh, I, __
dark - est night, __ yeah, the | world hurts less when I'm | by your side, __ }

__ oh, I, ___ oh, I, ___ when you and I col - lide. | You bring __

__ me to life, ___ | yeah, you bring ___ me to life, __

you bring _____ me to life, _____

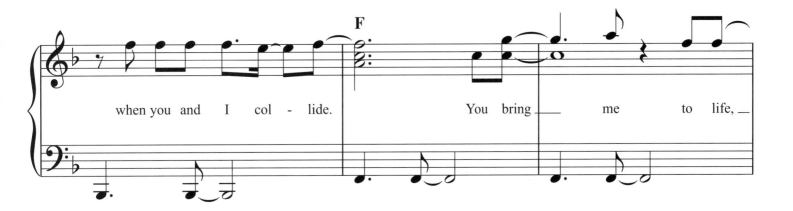

when you and I col - lide. You bring _____ me to life, _____

_____ yeah, you bring _____ me to life, _____ you bring _____

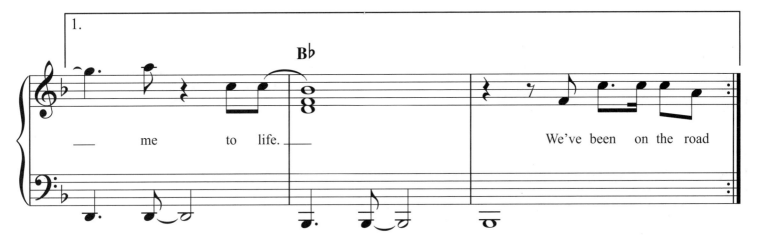

_____ me to life. _____ We've been on the road

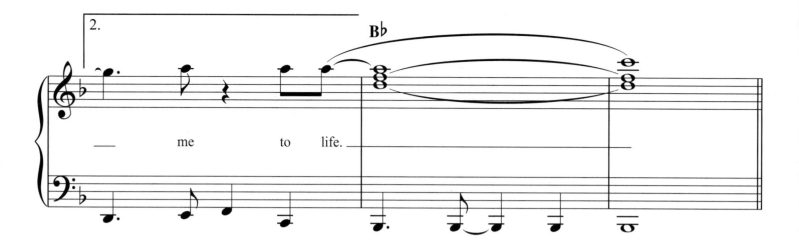

me to life.

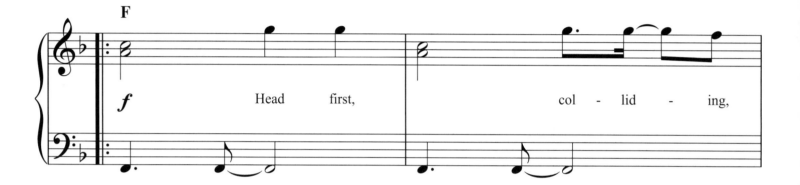

Head first, col - lid - ing,

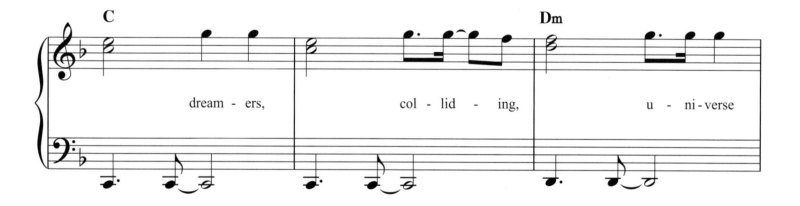

dream - ers, col - lid - ing, u - ni - verse

col - lid - ing, your love let the light in.

48

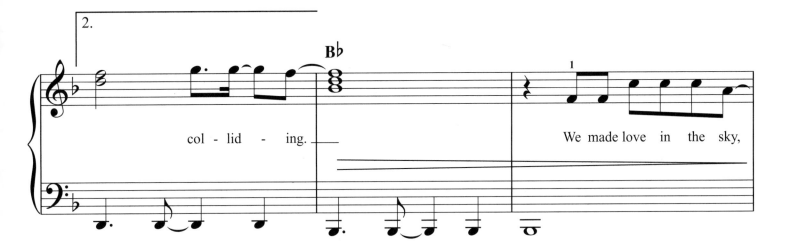

col - lid - - ing. We made love in the sky,

o - ver - slept and missed the North - ern __ Lights,

you lost your wed - ding ring but I did - n't mind

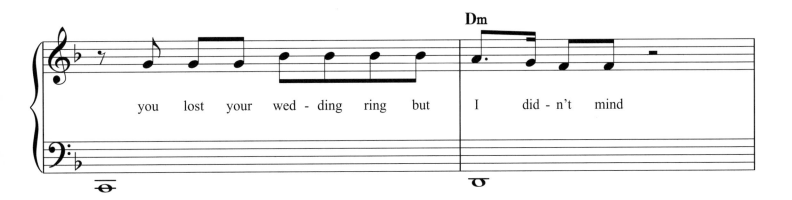

'cause I got a feel - ing, ba - by, we'll be fine.

2step

Words and Music by Ed Sheeran, Andrew Wotman, David Hodges and Louis Bell

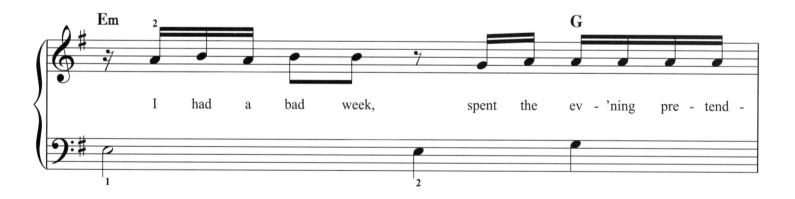

I had a bad week, spent the ev - 'ning pre - tend -

ing it was - n't that deep. You could see in my eyes __

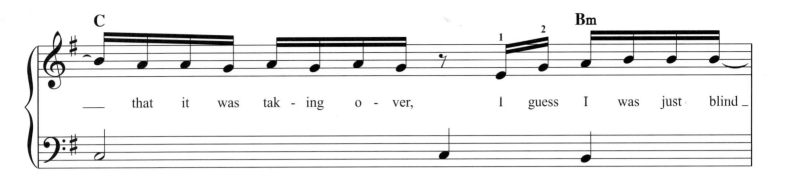

that it was tak - ing o - ver, I guess I was just blind

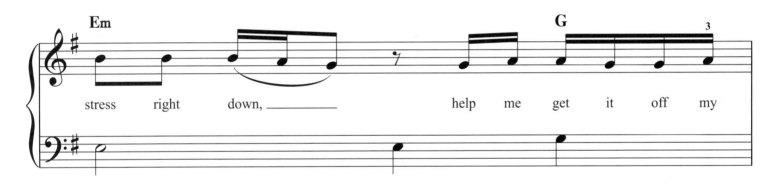

and caught up in the mo - ment. You know you take all of my

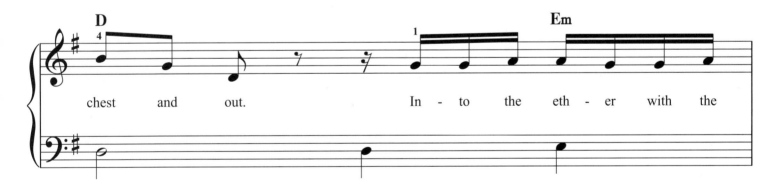

stress right down, _____ help me get it off my

chest and out. In - to the eth - er with the

rest of this mess that just keeps us de - pressed, we for -

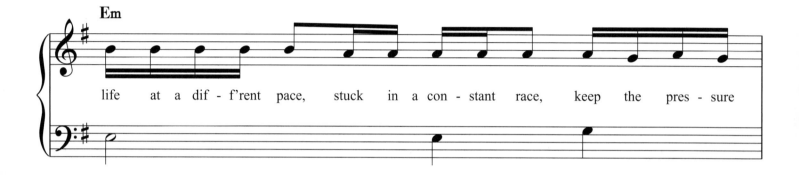

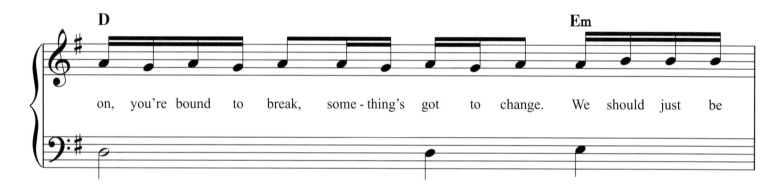

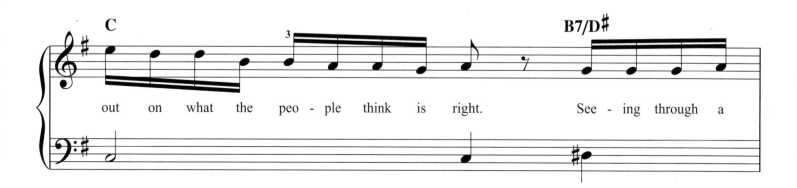

pic - ture be - hind the screen and for - get to be, lose the con - ver -

sa - tion for the mes - sage that you'll nev - er read. I think may - be

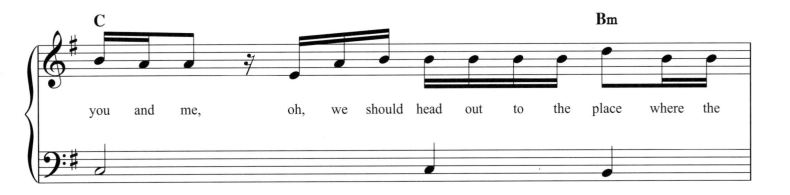

you and me, oh, we should head out to the place where the

mu - sic plays _____ and then we'll go all

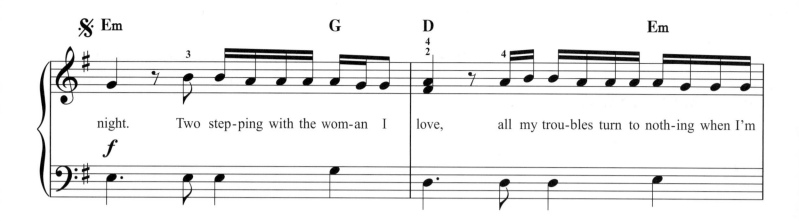

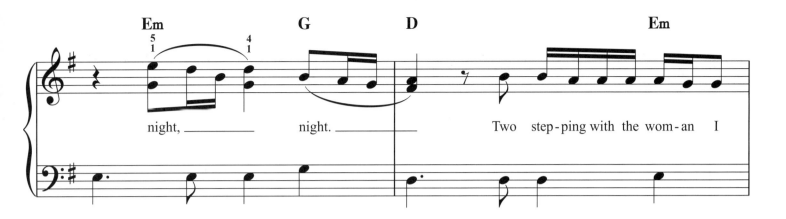

night, _____ night. _____ Two step-ping with the wom-an I

love, night, _____ yeah. _____ All we need is us, __ what do you reck-on, is it

just me? Words and weap-ons and oc - ca - sion - 'ly they

cut deep. Cri - sis of con - fi - dence, it tends to come when

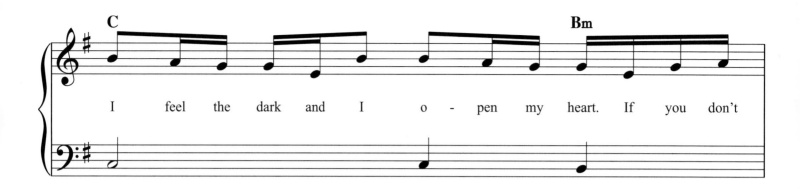

I feel the dark and I o - pen my heart. If you don't

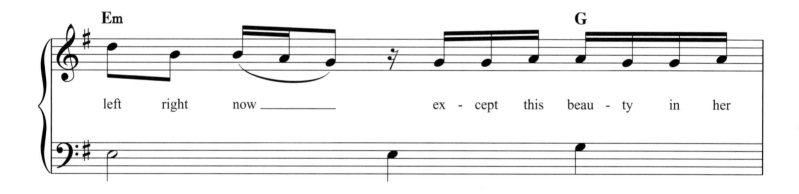

see it you should trust me, I feel like I've got noth - ing

left right now _____ ex - cept this beau - ty in her

dress right now. She got me feel - ing like the

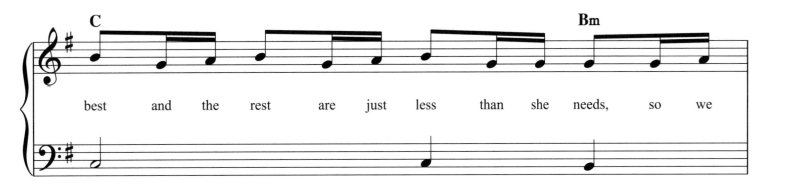

best and the rest are just less than she needs, so we

press play and step to the beat. 'Cause we're liv - ing

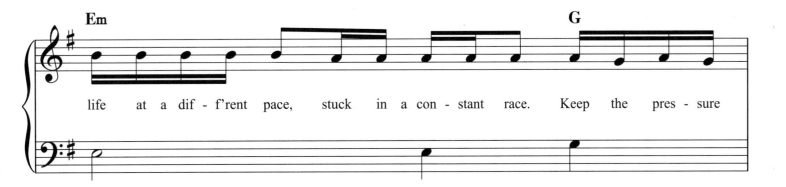

life at a dif - f'rent pace, stuck in a con - stant race. Keep the pres - sure

on, you're bound to break, some - thing's got to change. We should just be

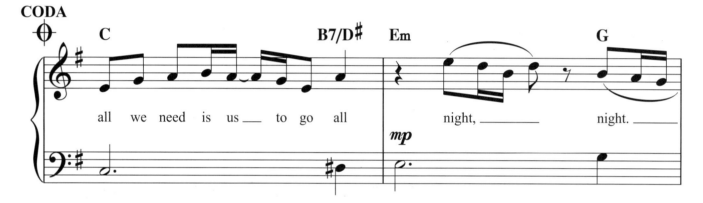

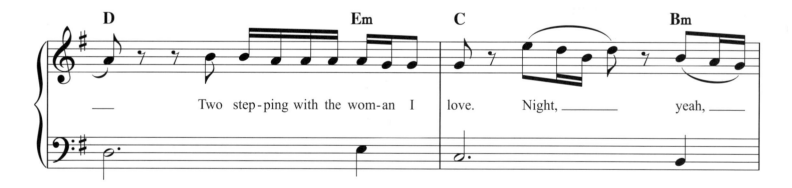

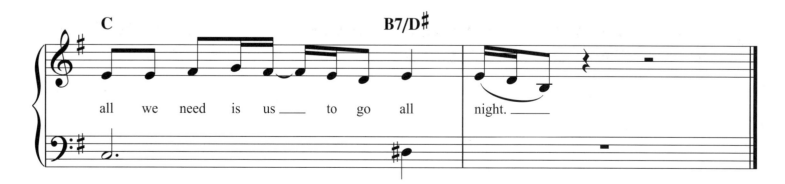

Stop The Rain

Words and Music by Ed Sheeran

Fast, driving pop

An - oth - er hu - man cloud to bring you down when you

blew the last ____ a - way and bring out a

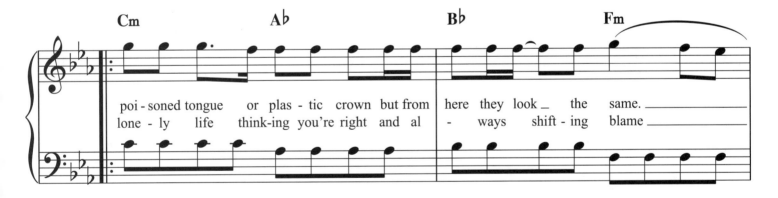

poi - soned tongue or plas - tic crown but from here they look ___ the same. ____

lone - ly life think-ing you're right and al - ways shift - ing blame ____

Some - times, it can get all too much for me ____ and that's

Ev - 'ry time it's get-ting more and more ug - ly ____ and that's

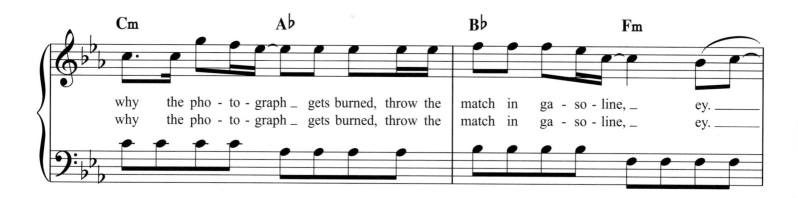

why   the pho - to - graph _ gets burned, throw the | match in ga - so - line, _   ey. _____
why   the pho - to - graph _ gets burned, throw the | match in ga - so - line, _   ey. _____

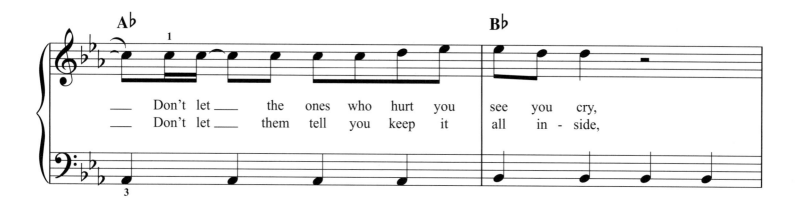

_ Don't let ____ the ones who hurt you | see you cry,
_ Don't let ____ them tell you keep it | all in - side,

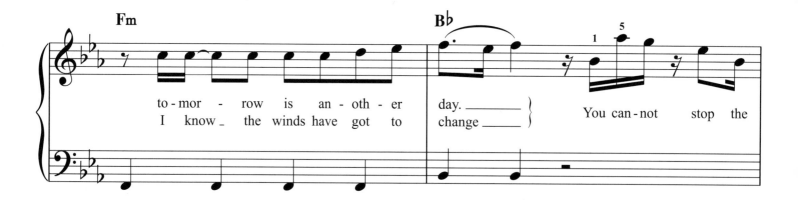

to - mor - row is an - oth - er | day. _____ } | You can - not stop the
I know _ the winds have got to | change _____ } |

rain, no way, | hold - ing an um - brel - la when the grey clouds   come

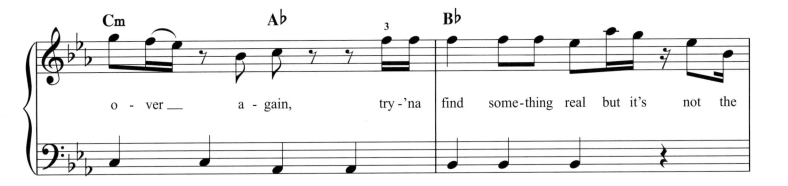

o - ver ___ a - gain, try -'na find some-thing real but it's not the

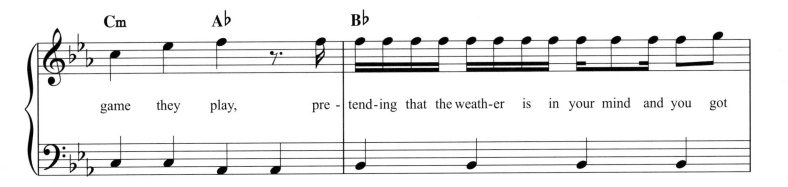

game they play, pre - tend-ing that the weath-er is in your mind and you got

no one ___ to blame but that's just the way ___ I feel. You can-not stop the

rain, yeah, yeah, yeah, yeah. You can - not stop the

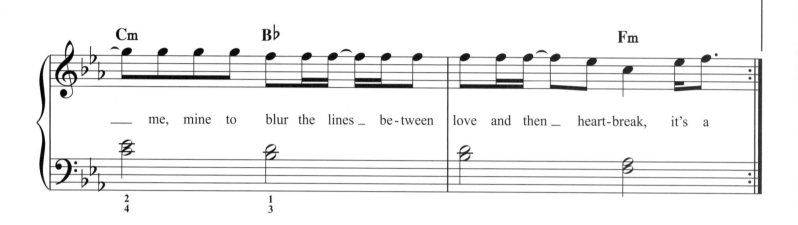

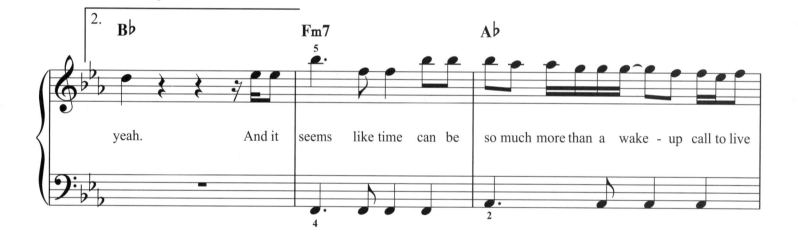

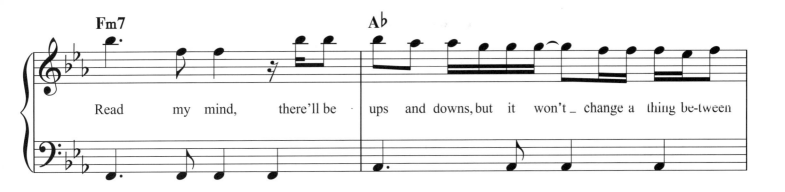

Read my mind, there'll be ups and downs, but it won't change a thing be-tween

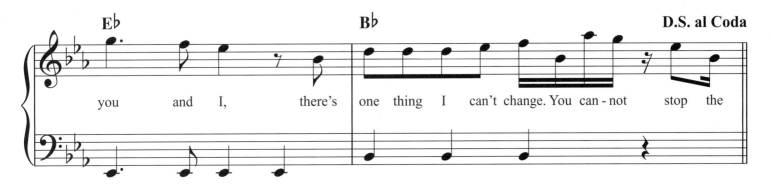

you and I, there's one thing I can't change. You can-not stop the

D.S. al Coda

CODA

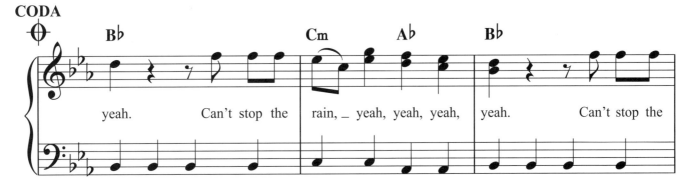

yeah. Can't stop the rain, yeah, yeah, yeah, yeah. Can't stop the

rain yeah, yeah, yeah, yeah. Can't stop the rain, yeah, yeah, yeah,

yeah. Can't stop the rain, yeah, yeah, yeah, yeah.

Love In Slow Motion

Words and Music by Ed Sheeran, Johnny McDaid and Natalie Hemby

It's been a while ___ since we've been a - lone, ___
It's been a while since it was you and me, ___

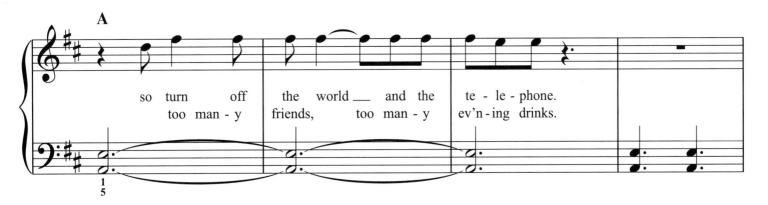

so turn off the world ___ and the te - le - phone.
too man - y friends, too man - y ev'n - ing drinks.

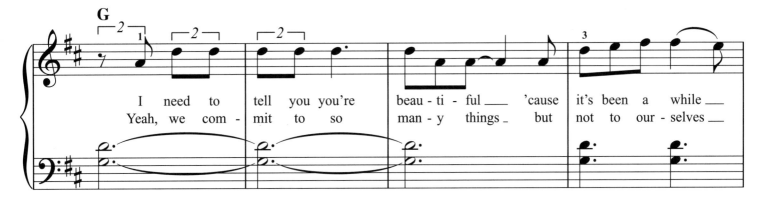

I need to tell you you're beau - ti - ful ___ 'cause it's been a while ___
Yeah, we com - mit to so man - y things ___ but not to our - selves ___

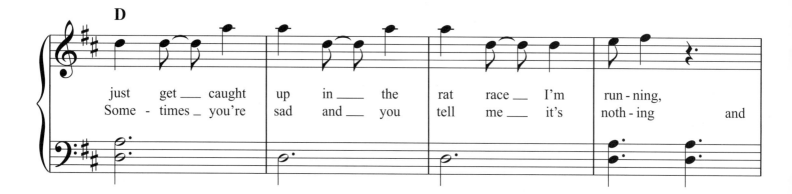

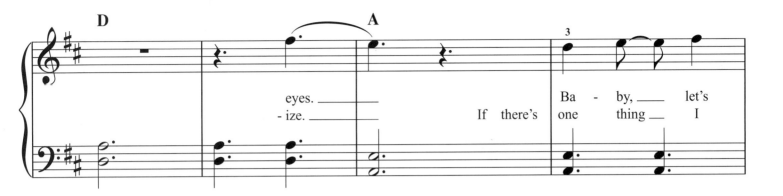

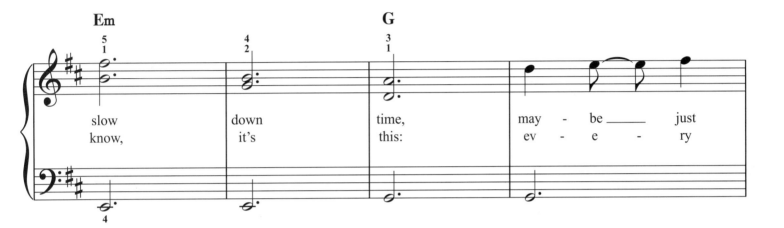

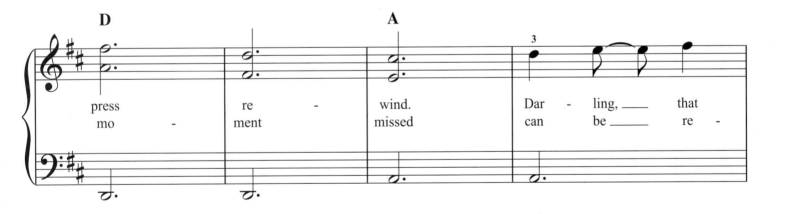

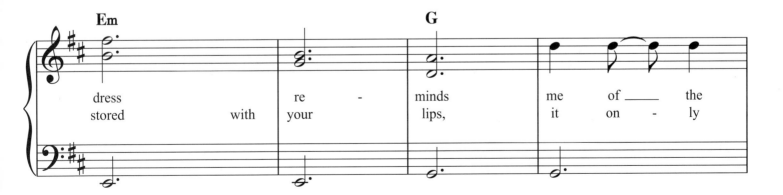

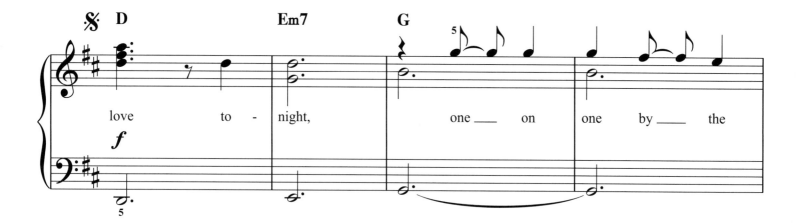

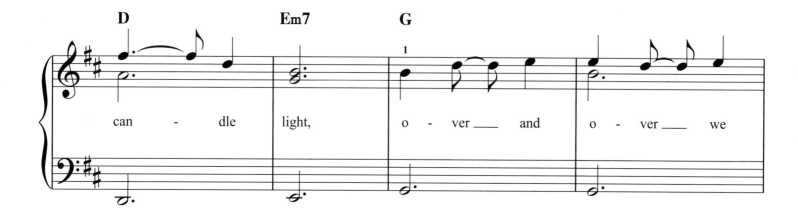

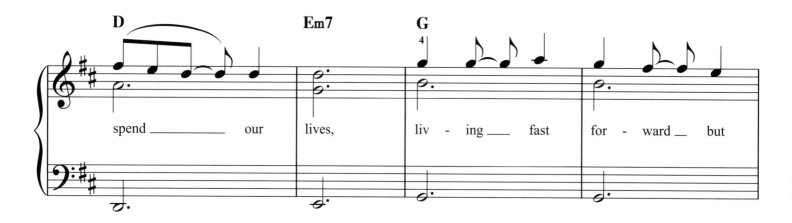

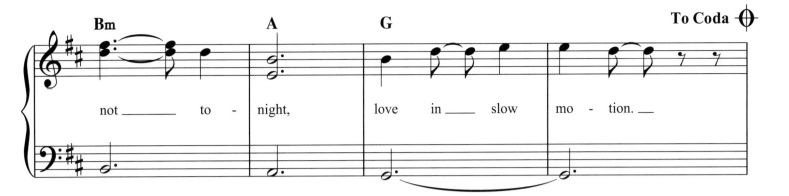

not _____ to - night, love in ____ slow mo - tion. ____

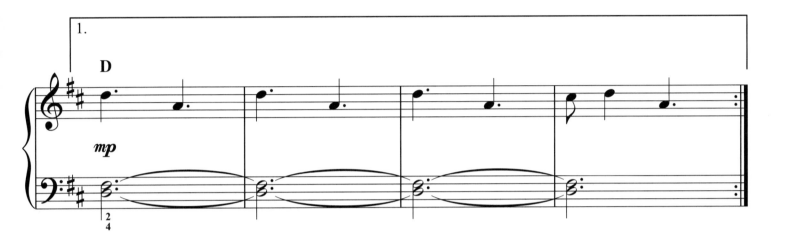

1.

mp

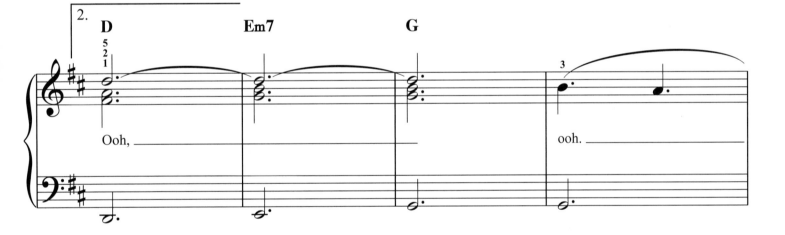

2.

Ooh, _____ ooh. _____

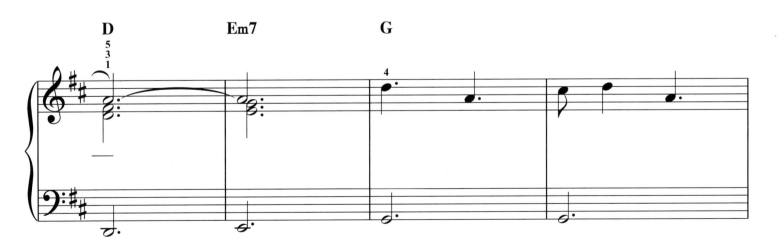

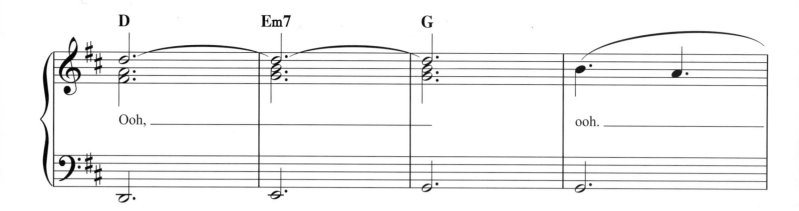

Ooh, _____ ooh. _____

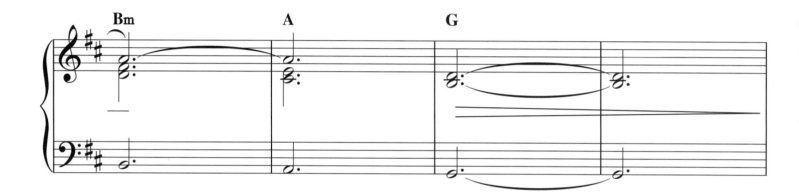

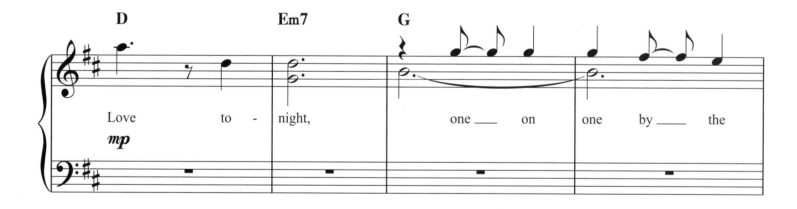

Love   to - night,   one ___ on   one by ___ the

mp

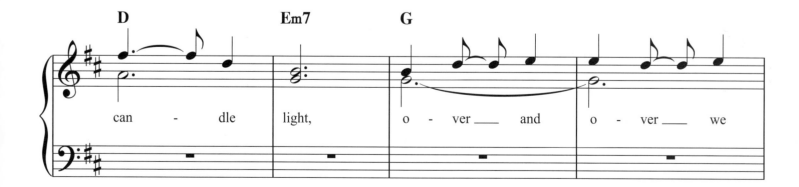

can - dle   light,   o - ver ___ and   o - ver ___ we

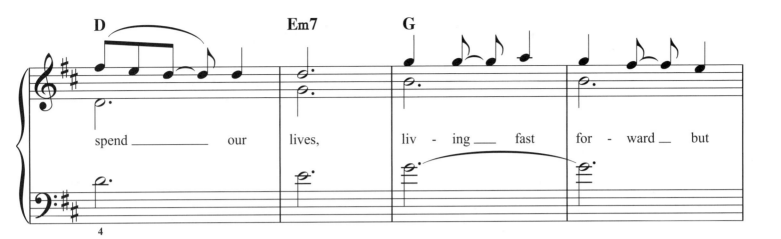

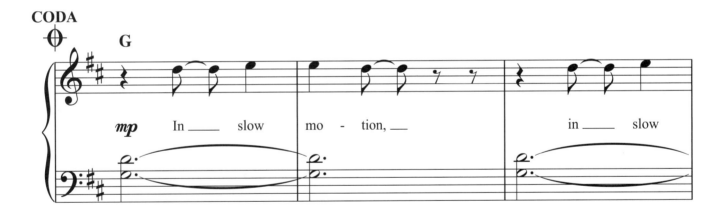

Visiting Hours

Words and Music by Ed Sheeran, Johnny McDaid, Amy Wadge, Anthony Clemons Jr., Kim Lang Smith, Michael Pollack and Scott Carter

Slow ballad

I wish that hea - ven had vis - it - ing ho-
- ven had vis - it - ing ho-
- ven had vis - it - ing ho-

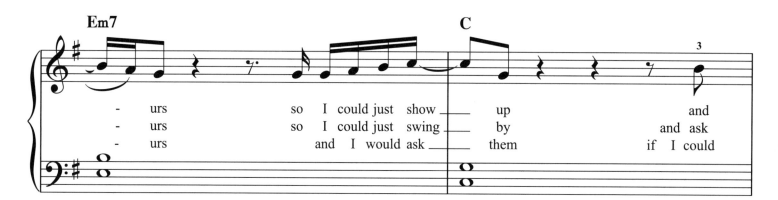

- urs so I could just show ___ up and
- urs so I could just swing ___ by and ask
- urs and I would ask ___ them if I could

bring the news, that she's get - ting old ___ - er and I wish that you'd met
your ad - vice, what would you do ___ in my sit - u - a - tion? I have - n't a clue
take you home but I know what they'd ___ say, that it's for the best, ___

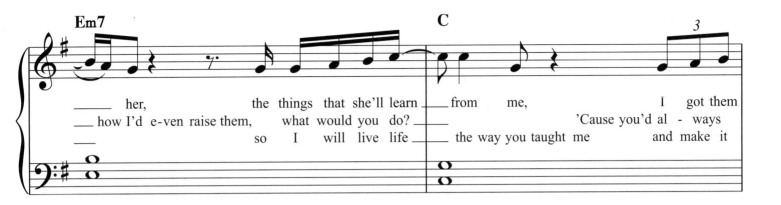

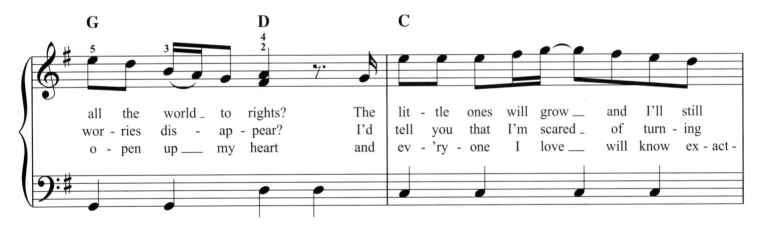

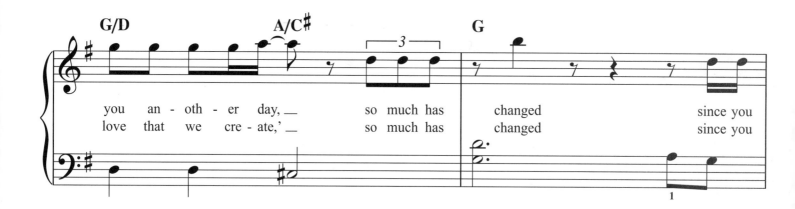

you an - oth - er day, ___ so much has changed since you
love that we cre - ate,' ___ so much has changed since you

been ___ a - way.
been ___ a - way.

I wish that hea -

Hmm, ___ hmm. ___

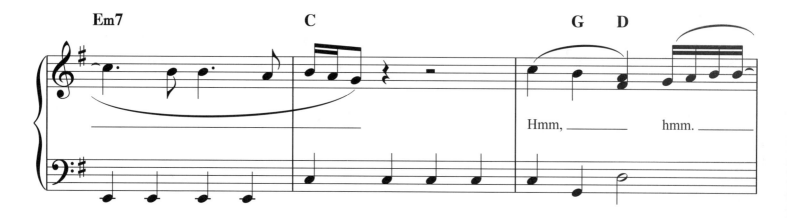

Hmm, ___ hmm. ___

74

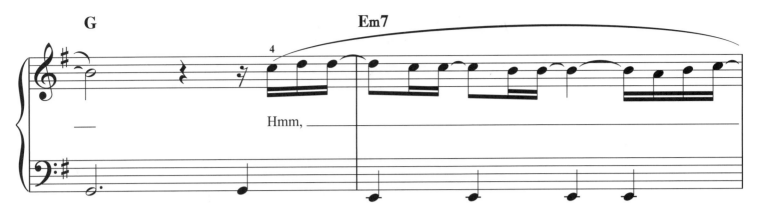

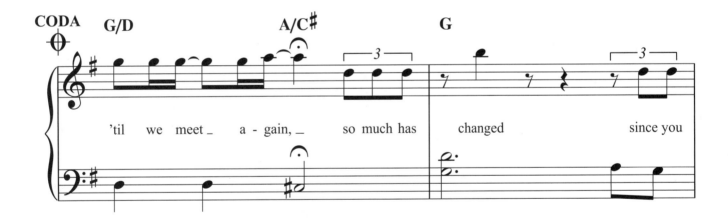

Sandman

Words and Music by Ed Sheeran and Johnny McDaid

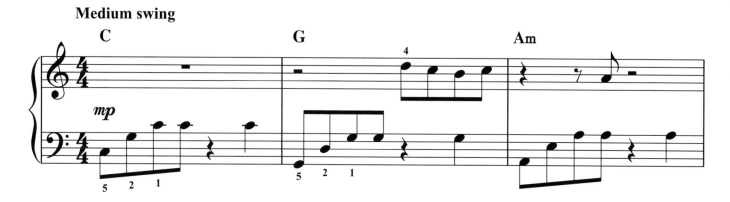

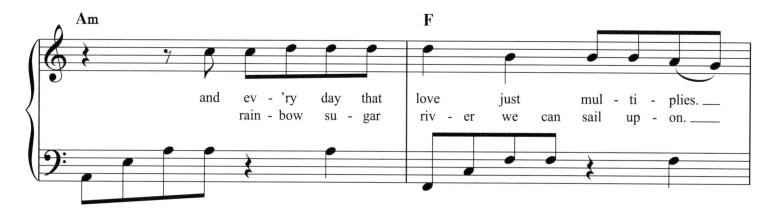

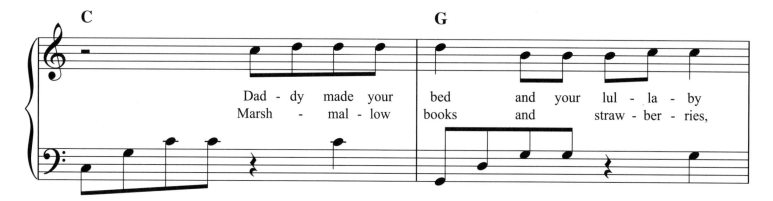

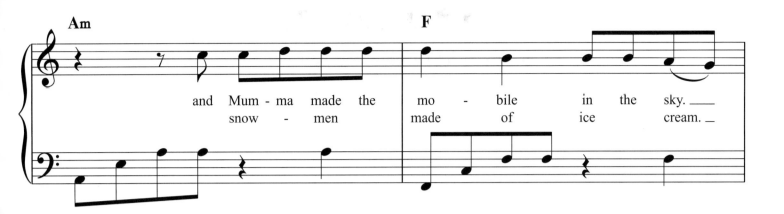

and Mum - ma made the   mo - bile   in the sky. ____
snow - men   made   of   ice   cream. _

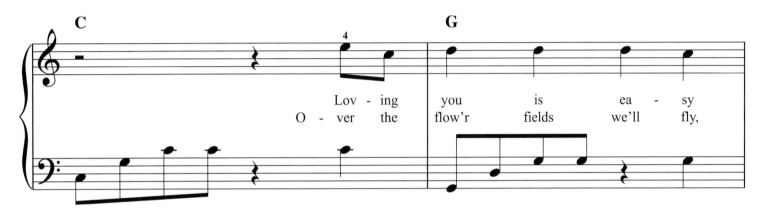

Lov - ing   you   is   ea - sy
O - ver the   flow'r   fields   we'll   fly,

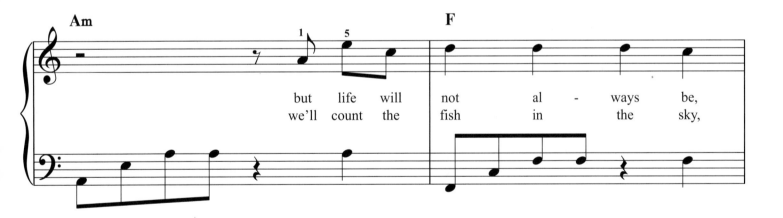

but life will   not   al - ways   be,
we'll count the   fish   in   the   sky,

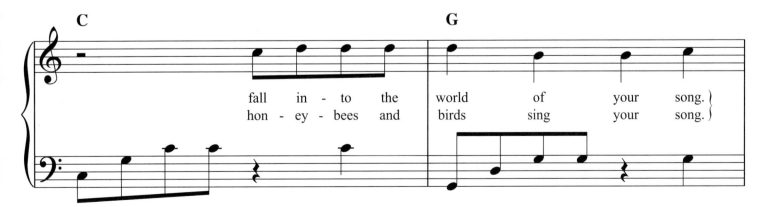

fall in - to the   world   of   your   song.
hon - ey - bees and   birds   sing   your   song.

What -ev- er you feel can nev-er be __ wrong,   come a-

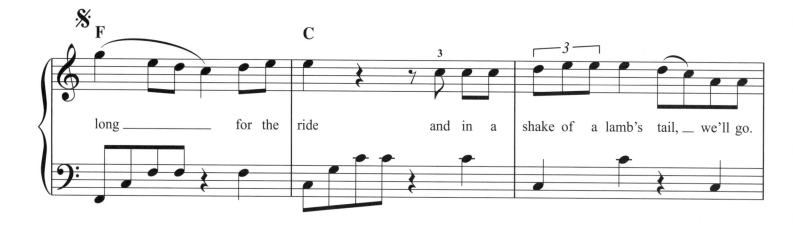

long _____ for the ride   and in a   shake of a lamb's tail, __ we'll go.

Be still, __   now ___ and close ___   your _   eyes _

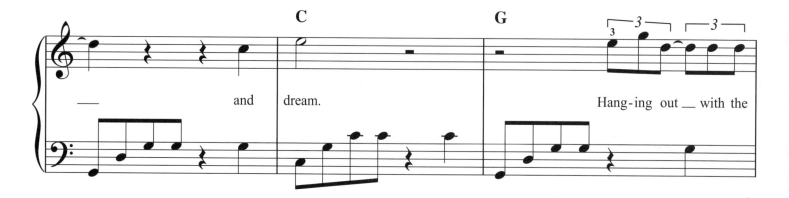

__   and   dream.   Hang-ing out __ with the

sand - man,   you look so sweet, ___ my ___ child,

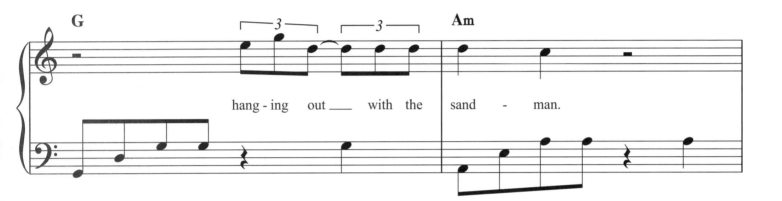

hang - ing out ___ with the sand - man.

Though there's rain out - side, ___ you'll be

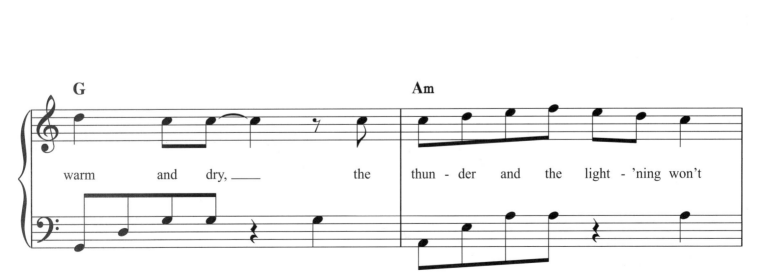

warm and dry, ___ the thun - der and the light - 'ning won't

hurt   you   now, ___   so   go   to   sleep, ___   my ___   love,

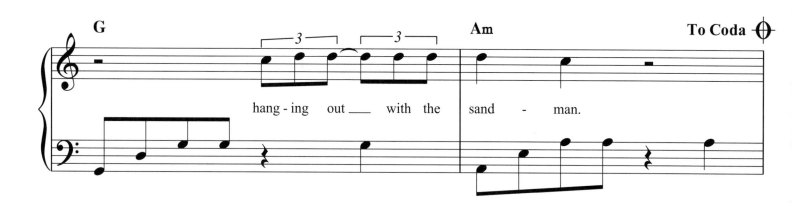

hang - ing   out ___   with   the   sand - man.

To Coda

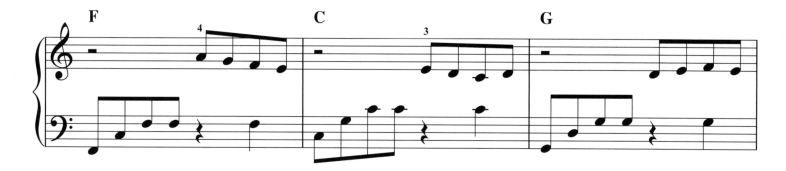

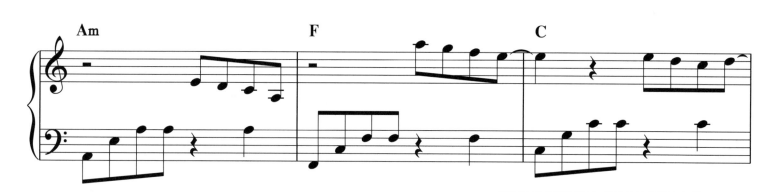

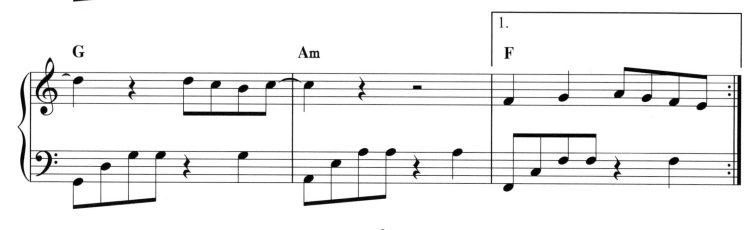

1.

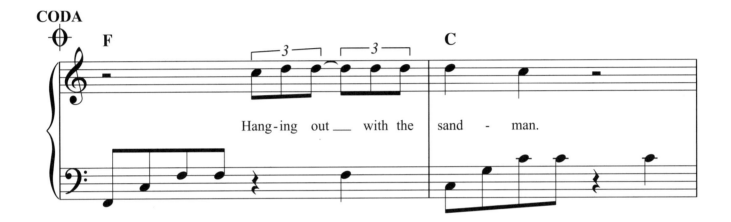

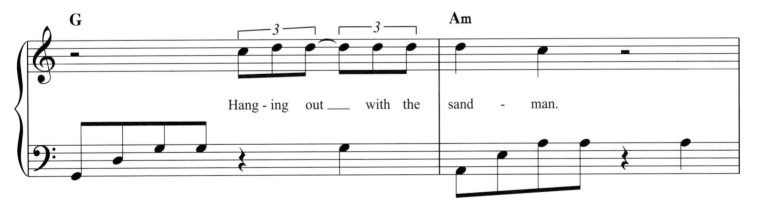

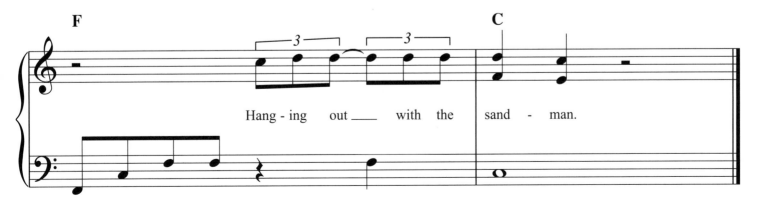

Be Right Now

Words and Music by Ed Sheeran, Johnny McDaid and Fred Gibson

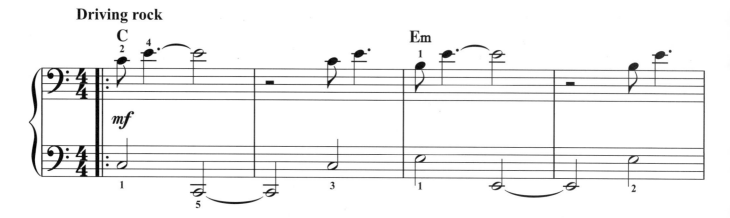

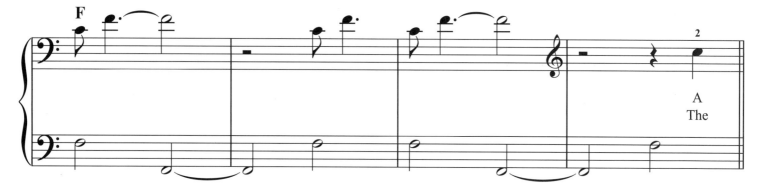

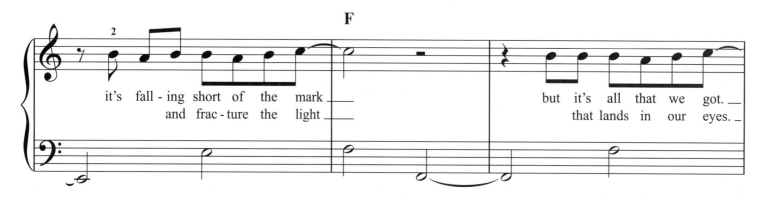

C

Ev - e - ry   tear   drop, ___
Ev - e - ry   mo - ment ___

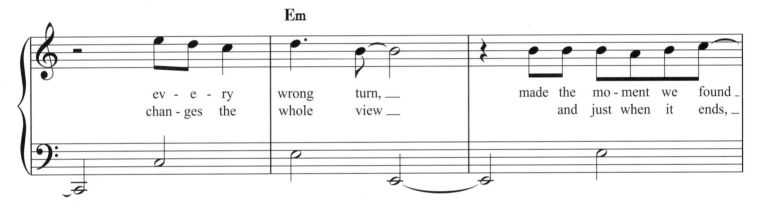

Em

ev - e - ry   wrong   turn, ___   made the mo - ment we found ___
chan - ges the whole   view ___   and just when it   ends, ___

F

and it's com - ing a - round, ___   a - round, ___   a - round, ___
I feel it a - gain, ___   a - gain, ___   a - gain, ___

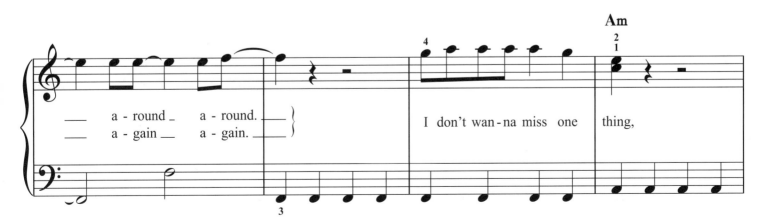

Am

a - round _ a - round. ___
a - gain _ a - gain. ___

I don't wan - na miss one   thing,

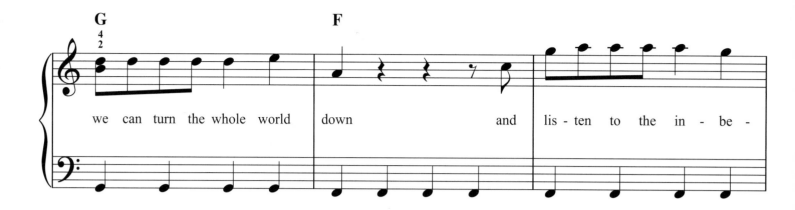

we can turn the whole world down and lis - ten to the in - be -

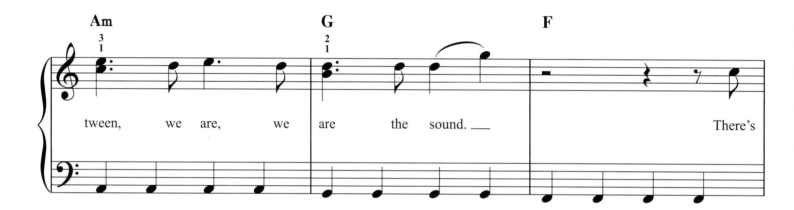

tween, we are, we are the sound. ___ There's

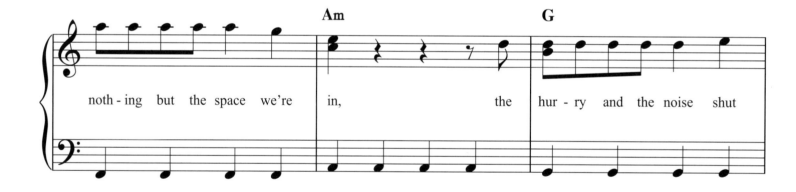

noth - ing but the space we're in, the hur - ry and the noise shut

out. Just stay here _ and be __ right _ now.

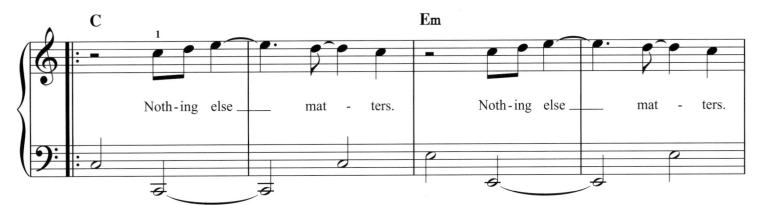

Noth-ing else _____ mat - ters. Noth-ing else _____ mat - ters.

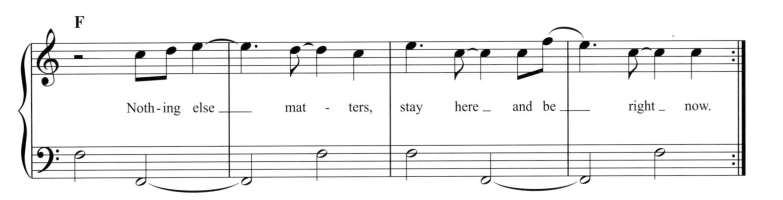

Noth-ing else _____ mat - ters, stay here _ and be _____ right _ now.

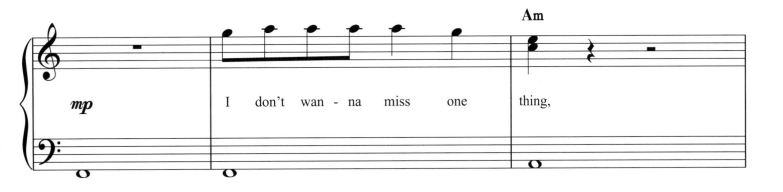

mp   I   don't wan - na miss   one   thing,

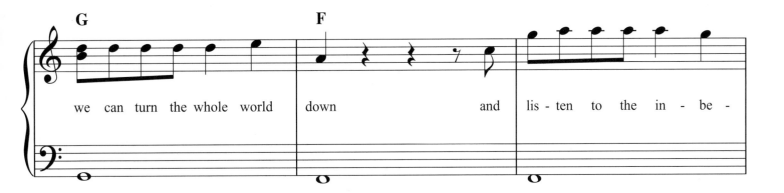

we can turn the whole world   down   and   lis - ten to the in - be -

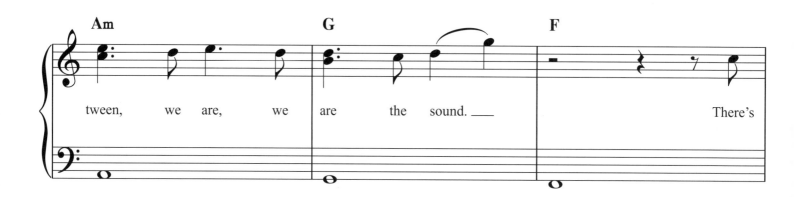

tween,   we are,   we   are   the   sound. ___   There's

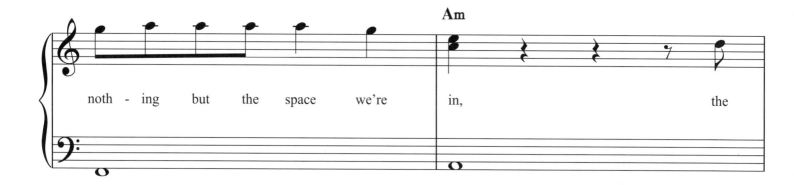

noth – ing   but   the   space   we're   in,   the

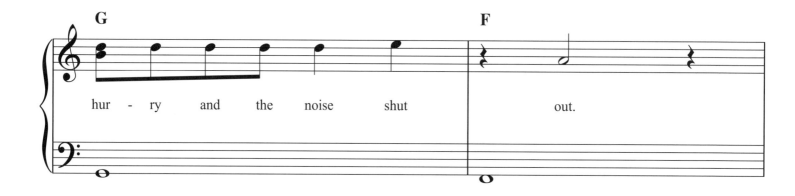

hur – ry   and   the   noise   shut   out.

Just   stay   here ___   and   be ___   right ___   now.